# THE FAMILY:
## Stronger After Crisis

# THE FAMILY:
## Stronger After Crisis
*by Paul Welter*

LIVING STUDIES
Tyndale House Publishers, Inc.
Wheaton, Illinois

Quotations from *The Revised Standard Version of the Bible*, copyrighted 1946, 1952 © 1971, 1973, are used by permission of the National Council of the Churches of Christ in the U.S.A., New York, N.Y.

*The Family: Stronger After Crisis* was originally published under the title *Family Problems and Predicaments*.

First printing, Living Studies edition, July 1982. Library of Congress Catalog Card Number 81-86693. ISBN 0-8423-0861-X, paper. Copyright © 1977 by Tyndale House Publishers, Inc., Wheaton, Illinois. All rights reserved. Printed in the United States of America.

**Part One
Problems and Predicaments**
Page 17

**Part Two
Anxiety**
Page 55

**Part Three
Hurt and Anger**
Page 97

**Part Four
Depression**
Page 135

**Part Five
The Struggle for Independence**
Page 169

**Part Six
Beyond Predicaments**
Page 201

# CONTENTS

Acknowledgments 7
Personal Introduction 9
Preface 13

1 When Family Problems Have No Solution 19
2 Problems and Predicaments 25
3 The Human Predicament 35
4 Learning How to Dialogue 41

5 Anxiety-Ridden Through Pretending 57
6 Humility: An Aid in Reducing Anxiety 68
7 Just As You Are 83

8 Hurt and Anger—Knowing the Difference 99
9 A Christian—Angry? 106
10 If He'd Just—Once—Listen to Me! 115
11 Getting Past the Bristles 125

12 The Dark Night of the Soul 137
13 Taking Action 145
14 The Gift of Involvement 160

15 Threatened by the Struggle 171
16 It's Hard to Let Go! 180
17 It Helps to Get Close If You Want to Get Away 191

18 You Mean a Parent Has to Be a Teacher, Too? 203
19 Receiving and Sending Silent Signals 220
20 If They Just Turn Out All Right! 234

Notes 243
Index 249

## Acknowledgments

The families, couples, and individuals with whom I have worked in a counseling setting have furnished me a reality base for discussing family predicaments. However, with the exception of two case studies, none of the illustrations used is about a particular person or family, but rather reflect combinations of several families or individuals. This was done to protect the confidential nature of the counseling relationship. The two persons in the case studies, referred to as Jerry (Chapter 6) and Ann (Chapter 12), gave me permission to use the material regarding them. I appreciated

## 8 : ACKNOWLEDGMENTS

getting to know my former counselees because each one taught me something about my life as they shared theirs.

The Faculty Research Services Council at Kearney State College awarded a grant which made it possible for me to complete the writing of the manuscript. I appreciate the support of the Council and the College in this project.

A number of friends and co-workers have given me help and encouragement as I've prepared this book and I am happy to acknowledge my appreciation to the following: Bernard and Marge Palmer, the Rev. John McNeill, and Jan Dorman.

I am indebted to former instructors and associates who have taught me how to work with people in predicaments. The late Dr. Edward John Carnell, former professor of apologetics, and president of Fuller Theological Seminary, a truly great teacher, differentiated the terms "problem" and "predicament."

Mrs. Martha Eisele, my supervisor when I worked as a counselor in Kansas City, taught me how to get involved rapidly with counselees and how to intervene when that was necessary.

Dr. G. B. Dunning, formerly a counseling psychologist in the Counseling Center at the University of Nebraska, Lincoln, and now in private practice at Greenwood, Nebraska, has been helpful to me in the special area of marriage counseling.

Lillian, my wife, has the very special gift of constructive criticism, a form of the gift of discernment. This is one of the most useful (and least appreciated) of all gifts. Because of this gift, and her willingness to work at it, she was able to make scores of valuable suggestions for improving the sense of the book. More than this, however, I am thankful for the life we have shared together for nearly twenty-six years. This life together—a gift from God—has been good.

## Personal Introduction

Someone has said that every meeting of persons is an exchange of gifts. I believe our exchange of gifts is that you give me your time and energy investment in reading this book, and I give you the investment of my time and energy in writing. I also believe I can't touch your life unless I in some way share mine. That's why I want to share some of my journey with you. I wish there were some way each of you could share yours with me.

In my Kansas farm home, I grew up knowing what love was, although I'm sure I couldn't have defined it.

## 10 : PERSONAL INTRODUCTION

But my parents loved each other. Oh, I heard them argue a number of times, but I saw many evidences of their love. One special scene during the last year Dad was alive summarized it all for me. They had been married for fifty-eight years. My wife, Lillian, and I visited them and I went first to see Dad in the Care Home. He asked me to take him to the hospital where my mother was at that time. So I helped him get into the wheelchair and took him over to the hospital. He said, "Just roll me up by the bed." He got close to Mother and reached out his hand. They held hands and looked at each other for several minutes before they said anything. It was beautiful to see. How grateful I was to witness the expression of their love that had grown through the years.

Like so many young people, I myself had found it very difficult to express to my family the love I felt for them. There was a time during my first semester in college when I was terribly lonely and homesick, and I didn't have enough money to go home on weekends. My parents came to visit me one Saturday, and I happened to be outside the house where I was renting a room. I was banging a tennis ball up against the garage door with my racket when I saw my parents drive up in the driveway. I just went right on batting the tennis ball for a little while, when what I really wanted to do was to run over to them and hug them and say, "Thank you for coming!"

That year I was searching desperately for meaning in life. I wondered where I had come from, who I was, and where I was going. Then in a beginning speech class, a young man who had been in the service gave a speech about his conversion. As he talked about the change in his life and what Jesus Christ meant to him now, it made a difference in my life and I decided to get to know him better. I talked with him after class and he invited me to come over Sunday afternoon. I went to Bill Cragoe's house that Sunday afternoon and most of the

## 11 : PERSONAL INTRODUCTION

Sunday afternoons that year. We had Bible study together, first just Bill and I, and then several other guys.

The next year I went to another college. In the fall of that year my cousin arranged a blind date for me. I remember showing up at the large Student Nurses' Home near the big hospital. I went inside and met the girl, who was rather scared. I was even more scared. Our conversation consisted mostly of vocal pauses for several minutes and finally she said, "Would you like to go to church tonight?" So I said, "Okay," and we went. That night Dr. Harold Street, a missionary from Sudan Interior Mission, spoke, gave an invitation, and I went forward. Pastor Walter H. Werner showed me from the Bible how I could receive Jesus Christ as my Savior. We read together Romans 10:9, "Because, if you confess with your lips that Jesus is Lord and believe in your heart that God raised him from the dead, you will be saved." That evening marked a new direction in my journey. The student nurse and I dated a few more times, but our interest faded and we never saw each other again.

Later I met Lillian, who shared my interest in child evangelism work. I never really believed theoretically in love at first sight. But it happened to me. We were married after I went into the army. After getting out of the army I finished college and then went to theological seminary. We had two children by then and our family of four went to Los Angeles, California, from Kansas. I went to seminary, not to become a minister but to fulfill a personal quest. The quest was to study the Bible in depth, to find out if indeed it was authentic, and to look for purpose in my life.

At one point in our marriage, Lillian and I decided we wanted to save some of Dad's and Mother's life and love for our children and grandchildren. So we suggested to Dad that he write down his experiences—tell his story. Over the next several years, he filled five Big Chief tablets. It took me a year or so to arrange all the narrative material in chronological order and his philosophy in a logical manner, because he had written now and then as events triggered his memory. Lillian then typed ditto masters and did some art work. It turned out to be 100 pages long, and we made 100 copies. So we had 10,000 pages here and there throughout the house. Our children helped to collate the pages, three-hole punch them, and fit them into covers. My father's story went to each of his children and grandchildren, then to neighbors and other relatives, and a library or two. It was an important part of my own journey to help my father share his.

After I finished seminary, we came back to the Midwest to live and I began teaching in a public school and later became a counselor. I've been working for the last eight years in a state college helping prepare teachers, counselors, and school psychologists. Right now I see this as my mission—to work where people flow by me each day. They touch my life and sometimes I touch theirs. The journey is a good one.

—Paul Welter
Kearney, Nebraska

## Preface

Years ago I was trying to teach Bill, our younger boy, who was a preschooler at the time, to share and to be willing to let others go first. One evening he came over to where I was reading and said, "Dad, I've been willing to let Steve use the bathroom first two times today, and I've had enough of this willingness business!"

This episode taught me that parents may *cause* family predicaments as well as help *resolve* them. I have written the chapters that follow with the goal of helping family members cause fewer family predicaments and resolve more of them. The main idea is that there are many resources available *within* the Christian family to deal with a crisis. These resources can be used in such a way that the family will be stronger after the crisis than before.

The convictions I have about families and about the predicaments they get themselves into have emerged from two sets of written materials and two sets of experiences. The first set of written materials is the Bible. The Scripture provides an account of man's predicament and God's intervention. It also has much to say about families. The second set of written materials is the literature of psychology. Psychology, as a behavioral science, does not provide answers to man's predicaments, as does Scripture. It is useful, however, because it helps the reader discipline himself in the science of observing and studying human behavior.

The first set of experiences is as a husband and father in my own family. Lillian and I have four young adult children—Steve, Kathy, Sue, and Bill. As the incident at the beginning of this introduction shows, I am not an expert on the family. It may be that there are no experts, in the sense of being "authorities." My aim is to share with you what I've learned about families. I genuinely hope that some of you who read this will share with me sometime what you've learned about families.

The second set of experiences is that of counseling with children, youth, couples, and families over the last twenty years. These persons, for the most part, have sought help because of a family predicament. It is, of course, a sign of maturity to seek help when one needs it. However, many of these had sufficient resources within their family to cope effectively with their predicament several weeks, months, and in some cases years earlier, if they had possessed some additional awareness and a workable method to apply. I hope that the shared ideas and experiences in this book will help you to resolve family predicaments quickly and effectively and to strengthen the family in the process.

The predicaments that are discussed are those which have appeared most often in the marriage and family counseling I have done. Hurt and anger are presented together because they typically emerge together. Most of the chapters are in groups of threes. The first chapter of each triad defines and describes the predicament. The second chapter looks at the predicament through the eyes of the family member who is most involved in the predicament—for example, the anxious person. This approach is used to assist that family member to become more open to *receive* help. The third chapter in the triad looks at the predicament through the eyes of the family members who will *give* help. In the "Independence" triad, the second chapter is for parents and the third chapter is for teenagers—and, in some cases, adults—who want to become independent of their parents.

# ONE: PROBLEMS and PREDICAMENTS

*Problems have a solution so advice is usually helpful.*

*Predicaments have no easy or satisfactory solution so advice is usually not helpful.*

*Therefore, one needs to know what the situation is before giving advice.*

# CHAPTER ONE: WHEN FAMILY PROBLEMS HAVE NO SOLUTIONS

Tim was frustrated in his work as a department store salesman. Nearly every evening he came home upset. He felt the main thing he needed when he got home was fifteen to thirty minutes of "peace and quiet."

Meanwhile, Julie spent the day with three preschool children. At the end of her day she felt pressured and cornered. What she wanted was someone with whom she could talk "adult." Also, she wanted her husband to play with the children so she could prepare the evening meal.

Tim's and Julie's three children had played happily during the day. But now they were looking forward to having their

## 20 : PROBLEMS AND PREDICAMENTS

father come home. Each one wanted to be sure that he or she was still loved by Daddy.

Tim came home, opened the door, and headed rapidly down the hall for the den. He never made it. Marilyn, Denny, and Lori converged on him from different directions. One got hold of one hand, one got hold of the other, and the youngest grabbed his leg. Julie came out of the kitchen and said, "Whew, am I glad to see you!" Each of the three children started talking; all their sentences began with "Daddy" and ended with their attempt to share part of their day with him. Tim felt angry and guilty at the same time. Julie wondered why she felt alone with so many other people there. Lori said, "Daddy, why are you so rough?"

Tim, Julie, and each of the three children needed love, but they needed different expressions of love. Tim needed the rest of the family to give him some time alone for "depressurizing." Julie needed Tim to listen to her, talk with her, and take responsibility for the children. The children needed their father's expression of warmth and love. Is this a family problem? If it is, by definition there should be a solution. An onlooker may think of some action which looks like a solution. But the five people involved do not see a solution. They feel helpless.

Greg was angry. "Why do you have to be at church every time the doors are open? Three times on Sunday, once on Wednesday, and at least one or two more times during the week. If you cared about the rest of us, you'd stay home more."

Nola felt attacked and responded defensively, "If you cared about the spiritual welfare of your family, you'd *take* us to church!"

"I don't want to go. They've got me pegged as a backslider.

# 21 : WHEN FAMILY PROBLEMS HAVE NO SOLUTIONS

They're just a bunch of hypocrites!" Greg's voice was getting louder.

"That's not true and you know it!" Little Charles sat in front of the TV, pretending to watch Sesame Street, but he was really tuned in to his parents' loud argument. He felt torn inside.

Greg saw one "solution" to their problem; Nola saw another. Neither solution was acceptable to the other person. Could it be that when we try to force our solution on another family member, we just make the problem larger?

Thelma, age fifty-five, was talking to her best friend, Joyce. "I don't understand the feeling I've been having toward Gary the last few years. I started to have these feelings about the time he had his stroke."

"What kinds of feelings do you have?" asked Joyce.

"I feel a lot of impatience, and I feel like he's a different man than the one I married. He used to be kind and considerate, and our marriage used to be a partnership. Now I do all the work, and all he does is just sit there! I know I don't have any right to feel this way, but I do."

"It sounds to me as if you might be feeling some anger at Gary."

"I never thought of that. Maybe that's right. I do get mad at him once in a while. Sometimes I wonder if I really love him any more. When I think these things, I feel guilty."

Neither Thelma nor Joyce knew where to go with the conversation after that. Both felt there was more to say. 'Way down inside Thelma was a deeper, more nagging emotion than either anger or guilt. She was hurting. But the hurt was layered over by the anger and she was unable to deal with it.

The situation with Thelma and Gary doesn't fit the problem-solution pattern. In fact, Gary may not even be

## 22 : PROBLEMS AND PREDICAMENTS

aware there is a problem, and Thelma, who is hurting very deeply, sees no solution.

"I get up in the morning and go through the day without even thinking about it," Carl said wearily to his friend Gene. They were drinking Cokes on an afternoon break from their assembly line job. "I don't even remember what I did this morning. Tonight I won't remember what I did this afternoon. My wife doesn't understand why I'm this way, and I don't either. All I know is I feel terrible and things don't look like they're going to get any better."

Carl had stopped looking for a solution to his depression. He placed himself on "cruise control" at the beginning of each day, and permitted his awareness of his surroundings to rise only high enough to allow him to perform his necessary tasks.

Norma was a young mother whose daughter, Sheryl, was four years old. Norma and Clark differed on many issues in their marriage, but the most important one was how to discipline Sheryl. Clark favored frequent spanking and harsh scoldings. Norma used a soft approach and at times permitted Sheryl to be disobedient rather than discipline her. She accused Clark of being mean to Sheryl; Clark accused Norma of spoiling Sheryl. The situation gradually worsened. Whenever Sheryl was naughty and Clark headed toward her, she went running to Norma. Sheryl was becoming more and more confused, Clark more and more resentful, and Norma increasingly anxious. Norma began to feel dizzy and light-headed whenever she was nervous or fatigued. At these times she had difficulty with her breathing. She had a complete physical examination and no organic ailments were discovered. Her physician said she was suffering from

## 23 : WHEN FAMILY PROBLEMS HAVE NO SOLUTIONS

anxiety, and he prescribed tranquilizers. Norma felt her crisis was deepening, and she didn't know where to turn.

Norma grew up expecting all problems to have solutions. But what is the solution for anxiety? She was finding the old problem-solution approach wasn't working when she most needed it to, and her feelings of panic increased.

Ray and Wanda were parents in their early forties. Their daughter, Rita, seemed to be growing more and more distant from them. Wanda said to her friend Myrna, "Now that Rita has a part-time job it's going to be even harder to keep track of her." Myrna asked Wanda which was the problem—the job or the relationship. Wanda admitted that she no longer had a close relationship with Rita and that she did not know how to rebuild their relationship. A week later Wanda called Myrna to tell her that Rita had run away. Myrna went over and sat down with Wanda and Ray, who said they knew where Rita was and they were sure she would be home in a day or two. Their real problem was that *they* didn't know what to do when she came home. Should they scold her, ground her, or should they welcome her back and hug her? They wanted to do both.

How can a problem have two equal and opposite solutions? Ray and Wanda felt like parents who have finally found their lost child in a large department store—they didn't know what to do with their own conflicting emotions. Is it possible that our time-honored method of using a problem-solution approach when things go wrong in the family is not workable, and may even make things worse?

Dave was extremely competitive with Becky. Whenever they discussed any issue, the conversation was likely to end in an argument. Dave was logical and analytical. He had been

## 24 : PROBLEMS AND PREDICAMENTS

in debate classes in high school and college and had learned to argue without getting angry. Becky tired easily of the competition and of the arguing. She often became very angry. Dave competed even with his children and would never give up once he had taken a position about some issue. He never allowed the other person the last word. He was aware he was doing this and didn't like it, but he didn't know how to change his style of communication. Becky was aware that the competition factor made her angry, but she didn't know how to keep from getting hooked emotionally once the conversation began. The family members were becoming tense and edgy. Sometimes Dave and Becky avoided talking to each other in order to prevent an argument.

The only apparent solution to this problem was to back off from it. But failing to resolve a conflict always worsens the situation. *Dave and Becky's solution failed, as did all the other solutions mentioned above, because there was no problem. And solutions work only for problems.*

All of those family situations were *predicaments*. And predicaments, by definition, have no easy or satisfactory solution. *The typical problem-solution approach is absolutely unworkable in a predicament.* Problems can be solved with information. Sometimes this information is called advice. But information alone, even well-meaning advice, is never sufficient to resolve a predicament.

How can you tell the difference between a family problem and a family predicament? And how can you go about getting out of a family predicament? What works? Are there ways to resolve family predicaments so that the family members emerge more whole than they were before the predicament began?

It is the purpose of this book to answer these questions.

# CHAPTER TWO: PROBLEMS AND PREDICAMENTS

The parents looked for Ken, their junior-high-age boy, inside and outside of church following an evening meeting. Finally one of them looked up and spotted him in a tree, some distance from the parking lot, where the rest of the youth had gathered. Later Ken told his story. Several of the boys had been playing after church and Ken, who was growing rapidly, suddenly discovered that the seat of his pants had ripped out. A friend tried to help him by saying, "It's no big deal; if you ignore it, other people won't even notice it." But Ken had shinnied up the nearest tree he could find—and wondered why it was taking to long to get dark.

His friend thought he could help Ken by giving him some advice. However, Ken didn't buy the advice. As a matter of fact, he came to the conclusion that his friend didn't really understand the situation at all! Now if the incident that Ken was involved in had been a problem situation, such as having a tear in his shirt, his friend's advice might have helped. But Ken was in a predicament, and advice typically doesn't help in a predicament.

## The Difference

There is, then, a considerable difference between having a *problem* and being in a *predicament*.[1] The term "problem," whether applied to a mathematical problem or a personal problem, implies there is a solution. All that is needed is to come up with the correct insight or enough knowledge and apply this solution to the problem. Another idea of the term "problem" is that it is something one person can solve for another. If a girl is baking a triple batch of cookies, she may seek help from her mother in getting the measurements right. This is a *problem* situation because another person can give helpful advice or directions.

A predicament, on the other hand, suggests a difficult situation offering *no* satisfactory solution. Another important difference is that a predicament is characterized by uniqueness, rather than by the commonality that characterizes a problem. A person who is in a predicament is *alone* in that situation. No one else's situation is exactly like his, at least not from his point of view.

Another key difference between a problem and a predicament is that the helper must already have built, or be willing to build, a relationship with the involved person in a predicament situation. For example, if a teacher knows a child

## 27 : PROBLEMS AND PREDICAMENTS

who has vision problems, she can suggest to the parents that they have an eye examination done and get glasses, if necessary. In most cases this is a problem that is easily solved. However, if the parents do not have enough money to obtain the examination and glasses, and if they refuse to accept financial help, the problem becomes a predicament. Anyone who wishes to help in this situation must be willing to invest time to build an involvement with the family, in order to earn the right to intervene.

Sometimes we as parents may cut off a relationship with a child because of a predicament he is in, and thus cut off ourselves from helping him. An example of a parent who made sure the family relationship was maintained was reported recently in an Associated Press article about Billy Graham.

> "We're very fortunate that all five of our children have followed Christ," says Graham.
> "The elder of the two sons, William Franklin, Jr., got off to a rocky start.
> "He was into everything you can think of, even having the police chief chasing him," says Graham. "I never got after him. Love would always come first. During this time, he would always hug and kiss me when he saw me. When it was over, there was nothing to reestablish."
> At his wedding, the namesake of the famed preacher had a surprise for his parents. He announced that he and his wife were dedicating their lives to Christ.[2]

This article doesn't seem to be saying that Billy Graham didn't believe in discipline. His messages and books show that he does. The point is, rather, that after his boy had grown up and had chosen to get into activities that his father disagreed with, his father still kept the personal involvement strong. As a result, his son's homecoming was like that of the prodigal son; the relationship was still there.

Sometimes it is difficult to discern between problems and predicaments. As the school psychologist in a city school system, I was asked to help in a situation that involved a fourth-grade boy. He was a troublemaker and caused many problems in his school. On one occasion he tried to leapfrog over a line of pupils at a drinking fountain! The day I was brought into the picture, he had been referred for a bike rack "problem." When he got to school he could find no place to park his new bike, so he jerked one out that belonged to a first grader and put his bike in its place. When I met with the parents, I asked the father what he had said to his boy that morning.

"I told him, 'Son, this is a brand new bike; you get one scratch on it today and I'll give you the licking of your life!'"

Immediately I realized the lad had been faced with a predicament rather than a problem. He knew he didn't stand a chance against his father, but he could have defended himself against the first grader. The fact that he acted out of a predicament did not excuse his irresponsible behavior, but knowing that fact did help the adults around him better understand his action.

The fact also came out that the father was setting up a massive predicament for his son. The father said, "I already have my boy's life planned. He'll take all the math and physics he can in school, in college he'll get undergraduate and graduate degrees in engineering, and then he'll become a successful engineer." The boy, of course, was already feeling pressured—trapped.

# 29 : PROBLEMS AND PREDICAMENTS

## The Importance of Knowing the Difference

We have seen that a situation takes on the proportions of a predicament when the involved person can see no satisfactory way out. He realizes he is trapped. The situation does not need to appear impossible from other people's points of view—*only from his*. When a boy or girl runs away from home, many parents are shocked. They knew their child "had a problem," but it didn't seem that serious. In many cases, if they had been more observant they would have realized their child was facing a situation from which, in his point of view, there was no good way out. In these situations many children panic and run away.

THE RUN-AWAY—IN A STATE OF PANIC

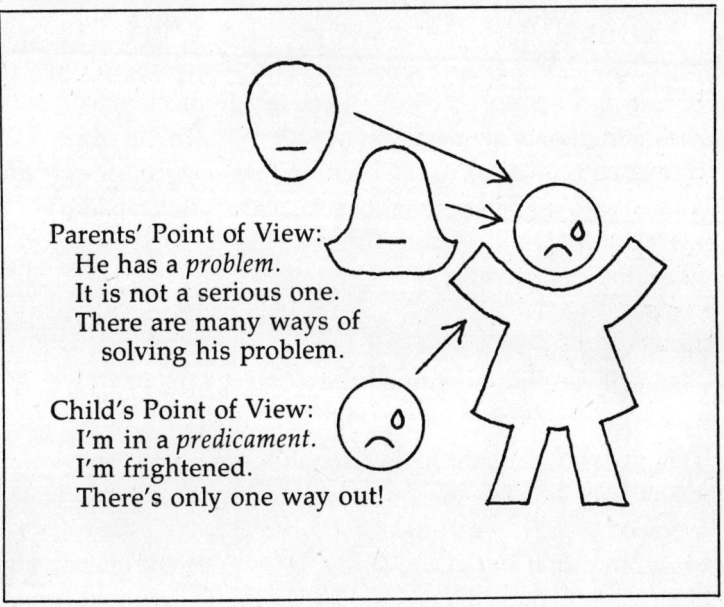

Parents' Point of View:
 He has a *problem*.
 It is not a serious one.
 There are many ways of solving his problem.

Child's Point of View:
 I'm in a *predicament*.
 I'm frightened.
 There's only one way out!

## 30 : PROBLEMS AND PREDICAMENTS

If we can become more aware of what makes up a predicament for other family members, we will understand the seriousness of their situation. We may get closer to the involved member by understanding he is hurting and by beginning to share his pain. Sometimes, however, we tend to respond with "easy" answers, and the other person knows we don't really understand.

One such easy answer is advice. We may give advice directly:

> "You should..."
> "Don't wait another minute before you..."
> "Why don't you try...?"

Or indirectly:

> "I found myself in that same situation once, and here is what I did..."
> "I've always found..."

But advice, either direct or indirect, usually doesn't help, because although problems are similar, predicaments are always unique (or always seem unique to the involved person). To the one immersed in the predicament, advice, even from the best intentioned person, comes across as cheap and powerless.

Another easy answer is reassurance:

> "Don't you think everyone has that problem?" (You're normal.)
> "Everything is going to be all right." (Not necessarily; it may turn out all wrong.)

The reassurance that he is normal doesn't help. The person with a bad headache doesn't feel relieved when he is informed that everyone has headaches at times. The reassurance that things are going to turn out all right involves making predictions that should be left to inspired prophets. I

## 31 : PROBLEMS AND PREDICAMENTS

remember the day, almost eight years ago, when I went out of the "reassurance business." One of my newly assigned duties as a college instructor was to act as advisor to a number of graduate students. My first graduate advisee was an able, sensitive elementary teacher who was beginning to work toward a master's degree in counseling. She and her husband lived on a farm. The first week of summer school there was a flash flood that destroyed some of their farm improvements and drowned scores of livestock. The financial loss was great. When she called to ask me to inform her instructors that she would not be in class for a day or two, she also said her husband was ill. Not knowing what else to say, I blurted out some reassurance, "Well, things can't get any worse." Two days later she called to tell me her husband had died. As I hung up the phone there were many thoughts and emotions whirling through my mind. One insight that came to me was that I reassured people because of my own need to help, rather than because of the need they had. I decided to stop this kind of helping; it didn't work.

In addition to advice and reassurance, laying a judgment on someone in a predicament is another easy answer. Someone has said that everybody complains about his memory, but nobody complains about his judgment. I have at times felt capable of providing a judgment on nearly every action under the sun, despite the Lord's clear injunction not to judge others (Matthew 7:1). Some examples of judgments are:

> "It sounds to me like you're blowing the problem all out of proportion."
> "The problem with kids today is..."
> "You couldn't care anything about us, or you wouldn't have..."

Judgments usually don't help because persons who are hurting need to be accepted, not judged. This does not mean we approve what they have done. It does mean we reach out to them in love, touching them in their own guilt and loneliness.

All these easy answers—advice, reassurance, and judgment—have as part of their intention the avoiding of sharing the other family member's pain, if in fact we are aware of the other's pain. The father who confuses his four-year-old son by saying to him, "Don't cry now; you are a big boy," (when his son is pretty sure he is still a little boy) probably has many thoughts and feelings churning inside, such as, "His crying makes me awfully uncomfortable"; "It isn't right for a male to cry"; "What will people think of me as a father if I let my boy cry over little things?"; "I'm feeling ashamed right now"; "If he would just stop crying, then I could stop hurting." The father's advice, or command, then, may be to lessen his own pain. Yet it is in being empathic (feeling with) another person that we learn to understand him, appreciate him, and come closer to him. And it is at this point the atmosphere of caring warms the family. This process of empathy has the added advantage that once a person has shared his psychological hurt with another person, he often can think clearly enough to begin taking steps to get out of his predicament himself.

## The Needed Resources

Inasmuch as persons don't resign their status as human beings when they make their decision for Christ, Christians face the same predicaments that non-Christians face. And Christian families are confronted with the same predicaments which confront non-Christian families. An important difference is that Christian families have additional resources to help them cope with the

## 33 : PROBLEMS AND PREDICAMENTS

predicaments. Many times, however, we fail to tap these resources, and we become ineffective in a crisis situation.

One of these resources is the emotional support that we receive from other Christians in our church or small groups. A person can't give what he doesn't have. Therefore, if we want to help another family member who is in a crisis situation, we must ourselves be emotionally supported by others. Emotional support refers to the help one gets from the affirmation and warmth of others. Karla was a woman who needed such emotional support. She was married to a "cold" husband. He had never learned to express effectively the warmth that was hidden beneath layers and layers of insulation. She found that her small Bible study group gave her strength and met her own needs for warmth each week so she could work at giving warmth to her husband, and thereby release some of the warmth in him.

Another resource is a study of the life of Christ. He was aware of others' predicaments—of the Samaritan woman and her fruitless search for love, of Nicodemus and the meaninglessness of his life, and of Peter who was caught in the predicament of his own declaration of loyalty to Jesus and his almost immediate denial of him. As we consider the life of Christ, we learn how aware he was of the needs disturbing the lives of those around him. We may find our own level of awareness increasing.

A study of other parts of Scripture can also provide important resources for the Christian trying to cope with family predicaments. I've found the Apostle Paul's letters especially rich in suggestions for interpersonal relationships in the home. Many times when I was about to "straighten out" one of my children (often when I was angry but couldn't admit it to myself until later), the words would come to me, "Fathers, do not provoke your children to anger, but bring them up in the discipline and instruction of the Lord" (Ephesians 6:4). The Psalms have been helpful in reminding me again and again that predicaments do come into a believer's life. In fact, the entire Bible speaks to the "Human Predicament," which is the root of all other predicaments.

## Questions

1. What is the difference between a problem and a predicament?
2. Can we help another person in his predicament if we are not involved with him?
3. Is there a member of your family you feel you are not really involved with?
4. How did Jesus help:
   The Samaritan woman in her predicament (John 4)?
   Nicodemus in his (John 3)?
   Peter in his (John 21)?
5. Is there a member of your family whom you have been giving advice to, and the advice isn't helping? Could it be he/she is in a predicament instead of simply having a problem? If so, what can you do about it?
6. Are you in a predicament right now? If you are, what is your plan for getting out of it?

# CHAPTER THREE: THE HUMAN PREDICAMENT

Why do so many "good" people feel so bad? Many people lead apparently good lives, but are moody and unhappy. One psychiatrist has reported that of all the people who consult physicians, only one-half have physical ailments which can be diagnosed, and that about one-fourth of all prescriptions are for mood modifiers—mostly tranquilizers.[1] Millions of people are hurting emotionally. Obviously, such a complex predicament has no simple solution. Yet because the situation is so closely tied to our subject—family predicaments—we need to tackle it head-on.

A little incident that happened to me gave me a glimmer of

insight about a remedy for my "down" feelings. Several years ago when my mother was still living, I had been putting off writing her a letter because I thought I was too busy. I said to Lillian one day, "I feel terrible about not writing to my mother." Lillian said, "Why don't you sit down and do it, then?" I couldn't fight with the logic of her question, so I sat down and wrote. I began to feel better as soon as I had finished the letter. The insight that grabbed me that day in a much more compelling way than it previously had was that I could begin to *feel* better by beginning to *do* better. Another way of putting it was that I discovered I could elevate my moods by taking some appropriate action. The action needed to be specifically related to the cause of the "downer."

## The Importance of Action

In some predicaments we don't *feel* like doing anything. We may want to avoid a touchy situation, we may not wish to admit we were wrong, or we may want to keep on with something we are doing, even though we know it's wrong. At these points of immobilization, we need to commit ourselves to take the necessary action.

Dr. William Glasser, in his book *Reality Therapy*, has emphasized the importance of action over feelings.[2] He sees his job as helping his clients take responsible action, rather than just helping them feel better. This approach, in a paradoxical way, often helps people feel better. Does one wake up feeling better about himself and then make a positive change in the way he does things? Or does one take some necessary actions and then feel better about himself? My own experience and my observation of persons who come for counseling indicate that it is usually the latter. We learn to elevate our moods by beginning to do the things we need to do.

The scriptural emphasis on action is present in many passages. One of these is Matthew 21:28-31.[3]

> Now, what do you think? There was a man who had two sons. He went to the older one and said, "Son, go work in the vineyard today." "I don't want to," he answered, but later he changed his mind and went to the vineyard. Then the father went to the other son and said the same thing. "Yes, sir," he answered, but he did not go. Which one of the two did what his father wanted?
> "The older one," they answered.
> "And I tell you this," Jesus said to them. "The tax collectors and the prostitutes are going into the Kingdom of God ahead of you."

Jesus did not ask the question, "Which one of the two *said* he was going to do the will of his father?" or "Which one of the two *intended* to do the will of his father?" Rather, he asked, "Which of the two *did* the will of his father?"

## The Human Predicament

We have seen that failing to take necessary action can put us in a bad way with God, others, and ourselves. On the other hand, doing something that is wrong can also have negative results. The nature of the human predicament is clearly stated by the Apostle Paul, "I do not understand my own actions. For I do not do what I want, but I do the very thing I hate."[4] It's important to note that the biblical statement concerns actions—and the lack of them. The focus of the Bible and the focus of psychology merge in spotlighting behavior. Psychology is the study of behavior. Thoughts, feelings, and emotions are important, but they cannot be observed and studied in the same way behaviors can.

The human predicament, then, is caused by our *failing* to

do many of the things we need to do and, on the other hand, *doing* many of the things we know we should not do. So—how do we begin to change the way we do things? Is there a pattern we can follow?

## God Took Action

To resolve the basic human predicament of sin—our failure to do the things we know we should do, and on the other hand, the violation of our conscience by many of the things we do—God took action. Jesus Christ came to earth and involved himself deeply in the human predicament. The Bible says he "went about preaching," and also that he "went about doing good." Then he took the ultimate action, giving his life to redeem us from our sin, and subsequently rose from the dead. The important thing to notice here is that when God was faced with resolving a predicament, he took *action*. Thus a pattern has been provided for us.

## Can We Feel Good All the Time?

If we take action to emerge from our predicaments, can we expect to have good, positive, happy feelings all day every day? I remember trying to work through this question of happiness after I became a Christian at the age of nineteen. Some of my newly found Christian friends gave me some literature to read on "The Victorious Christian Life." Reading this material really discouraged me. I got the idea that it was unchristian not to be happy all the time. Looking back on it, I'm rather sure that was not the point of the Victorious Christian Life Movement, but that's the way it came across to me.

About this same time another Christian gave me Hannah

## 39 : THE HUMAN PREDICAMENT

Smith's book, *The Christian's Secret of a Happy Life*. My reading of this book strengthened my idea that I should always be happy as a Christian. This made me even more unhappy. I wondered, "What's wrong with me?" My guilt started to skyrocket and I began to *pretend* I was happy.

Fortunately I got involved in Bible reading and Bible study. I noticed that the Psalms presented a rather wavy graph of a believer's feelings. Sometimes the Psalmist was up; sometimes he was down. When he was down, he said he was down; he didn't try to pretend he was up. When I moved into the New Testament, I found that the saints there, even after the resurrection, had their down times. Gradually it came to me that I could have a "normal" Christian life and not be happy twenty-four hours a day. My timing was off—I wanted something on earth that is only possible later, in heaven.

Well, when I found out I didn't *have* to be happy all the time, I immediately felt much better. It was as if a heavy burden were lifted. Since that time I have found other confirmations of this point of view. I noticed that even the Declaration of Independence doesn't guarantee the right to happiness—only the right to chase it! Another confirmation was reading what C. S. Lewis reported concerning Charles Williams's view of the problem of youth's pursuit of happiness:

> He also said that when young people come to us with their troubles and discontent, the worst thing we could do was to tell them that they were not so unhappy as they thought. Our reply ought rather begin, "but of course..." for young people usually are unhappy, and the plain truth is often the greatest relief we can give them. The world is painful in any case: but it is quite unbearable if everyone gives us the idea that we are meant to be liking it. Half the trouble is over when that monstrous demand is withdrawn. What is

unforgivable if judged as a hotel may be very tolerable as a reformatory.[5]

Williams states that situation in a somewhat bleaker way than I would. Yet his primary argument, that we will encounter pain, is realistic and unassailable. It is not unamerican to suffer, nor unchristian either. But the point is, there is no use to undergo unnecessary suffering.

To overcome the paralysis that keeps us in a predicament, it is necessary to take several steps. First, we need to make a commitment to change the way we are doing things—to begin to take action. We need to make this commitment to change whether we feel like it or not. This commitment is an act of the will rather than a result of our feelings. I wrote to my mother not because I "felt like it," but because I decided to. The next step after the commitment is to begin—to take the action. Finally, the good outcomes of our action usually make us feel better about ourselves, and this encourages and reinforces us in continuing to do the things we need to do.

## Questions

1. What do you understand the human predicament to be?
2. Which of the following is more characteristic of you?
   To violate your conscience by your actions?
   To violate your conscience by your lack of actions?
3. As you look back over this past week, what percentage of the time would you say you have been consciously happy? 90%, 75%, 50%, 25%?

# CHAPTER FOUR: LEARNING HOW TO DIALOGUE

We learn how to talk early in life. The average two-year-old can say about 200 words. By the time he's five and ready for kindergarten, he has developed a vocabulary of 2500 words. But in the give and take of conversation, in the exchange of ideas and opinions, in personal interaction—in *dialogue*—our learning proceeds at a much *slower* rate. Learning words depends on our intelligence and the amount of verbal stimulation we have from those around us. Learning to carry on a dialogue is much more complex and depends on additional factors, such as our ability to listen, our understanding of people, and our interest in and awareness of the person we are conversing with.

Is there a special way we should carry on a dialogue with a person who is in a predicament? It all depends on what our usual method is. We may have to change the way we talk. Many approaches used in everyday conversation result in talking about the weather, engaging in a series of monologues, or in some other way failing to meet the need of either person.

Let's take a look at a situation that is common to homes with school-age children or preschool children.

> There are two eight-year-old girls, Barb and Doris, in an argument. They get so mad they hit each other, and then they both run home crying. Suppose you had X-ray vision and super hearing and could observe them running into their own houses and yelling the same sentence to their mothers: "Doris (Barb) hit me and I hate her!" The mothers reply:
>
> *Barb's Mother:* "Barb! You don't really hate her."
> *Doris' Mother:* "It really hurt to be hit, especially by such a good friend as Barb."

Which of these responses would be a dialogue starter? Which would be a dialogue stopper? Which girl would probably stop crying first (providing they both felt the same amount of physical pain from the hit)? To answer these questions, we can apply three tests of an effective dialogue response: Is the response warm, straight, and strong?

Let's check them first for *warmth*. Barb's mother's response comes across as rather cold. This is because the response does not focus on Barb as a person; it focuses on a problem. The problem, from the point of view of Barb's mother, is that Barb is voicing hatred. This is unacceptable, perhaps

## 43 : LEARNING HOW TO DIALOGUE

because of a belief that Christians don't (or shouldn't) hate. Therefore, Barb's mother chooses this moment to teach her a lesson. She has the best of intentions and wants to help Barb, but the timing is off, because Barb is not in a receptive attitude for learning!

Doris's mother's response, "It really hurt to be hit, especially by such a good friend as Barb," is warm because it *resonates* with one of Doris's deepest feelings. By resonating, I mean saying back the deep emotion the other person feels. This tells Doris that her mother really understands "where she's coming from." Later we will work on distinguishing hurt and anger, two very closely related emotions. But for now, it's enough to see that Doris's mother focused on Doris, not on a problem she felt she had.

The diagram on the following page, "The Focus of a Dialogue," shows the importance of differentiating between a problem and a predicament. As we have learned earlier, a problem yields to advice and a predicament does not. Therefore, we need to address ourselves to the problem, if there is one, and to the person, if he/she is immersed in a predicament. It is crucial, however, that we don't mistake a predicament for a problem.

Let's make a second check on the response of the two mothers—this time to see if the response is *straight*. The response, "Barb! You don't really hate her," is a bent rather than a straight message. It is bent because it is wrapped around the real, unspoken message which would probably go something like this, "Hating somebody is a dreadful thing, and you are not to do it!" This message is confusing to Barb, because she feels at the moment she really does hate Doris. Furthermore, it doesn't accomplish its aim of taking away the hate. In fact, it may add another sin—lying (You don't really hate her).

The response, "It really hurt to be hit, especially by such a

## 44 : PROBLEMS AND PREDICAMENTS

### THE FOCUS OF A DIALOGUE

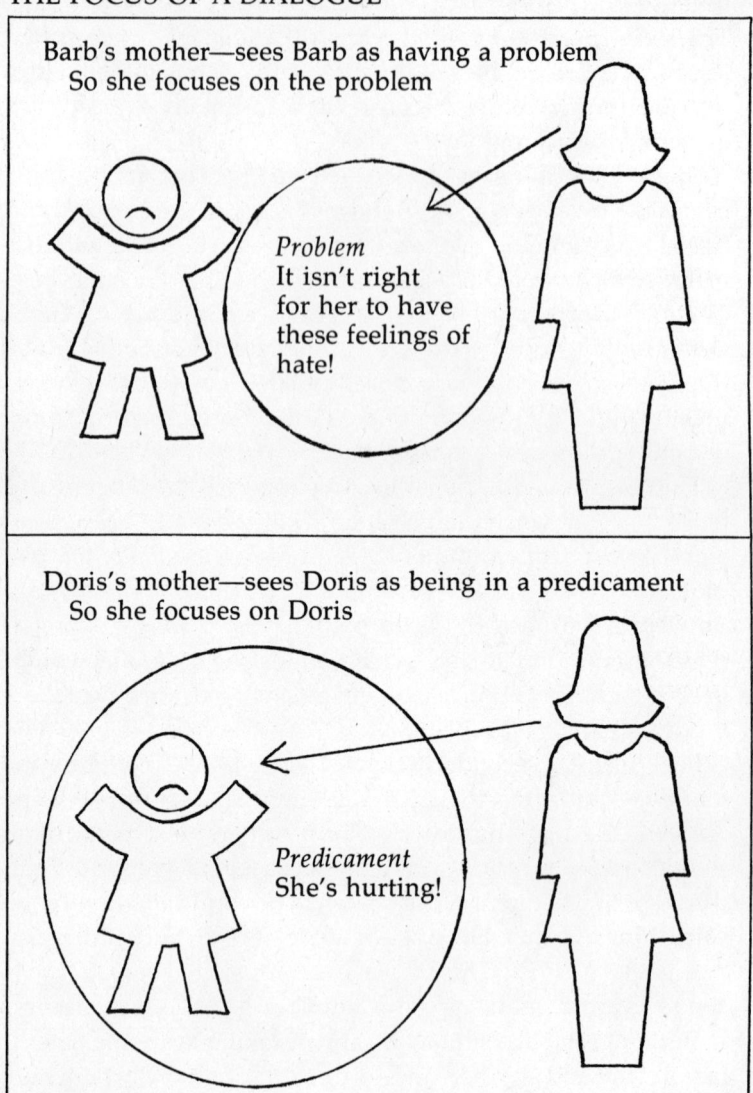

Barb's mother—sees Barb as having a problem
  So she focuses on the problem

*Problem*
It isn't right for her to have these feelings of hate!

Doris's mother—sees Doris as being in a predicament
  So she focuses on Doris

*Predicament*
She's hurting!

good friend as Barb," is straight because it describes accurately what is going on inside Doris at the moment. A straight answer tends to be a dialogue starter because it has a ring of truth to the other person.

A third test of a response is that it should be *strong*. A strong response is one that comes across with courage instead of fear. It says, "I'm willing to stand with you; I won't back off and leave you alone in your predicament." It is a little more difficult to test the responses we've been working with for strength than it was for warmth and straightness. However, we can see that the response which denied Barb's feelings was made, at least partially, out of fear. As you look at the diagram again, you will notice it left Barb all alone. Barb didn't feel any strength coming across. Rather, she felt unsupported. Doris, on the other hand, could probably feel the strength and support coming across from her mother. Doris's mother was saying, "I'm willing to be with you in your pain." Would this tend to make Doris cry longer? No. Usually when we feel deeply understood by another person, and when we know that person is emotionally alongside us, the psychological pain subsides much faster.

If you aren't sure about this, though, don't buy it. Give it a try and see what happens. If this way of carrying on a dialogue is somewhat different than the conversational style you usually employ, you will need both patience and perseverance to implement a new style. Some practical suggestions are given below for implementing the three helps for a successful dialogue.

## Responding with Warmth

To respond with warmth, in fact to respond at all, it is necessary to know what the other person said, and how he said it. This, of course, requires listening skills. When I began my counseling training, over twenty years ago, it didn't take long for me to realize I was an ineffective listener. So as a reminder, I chose Proverbs 18:13 as my lifetime counseling motto, "If one gives answer before he hears, it is his folly and shame." Through the years this verse has provided me helpful direction in counseling, and in daily living.

Paul Tournier has described quite succinctly the present situation with regard to listening:

> Listen to all the conversations of our world, those between nations as well as those between couples. They are for the most part dialogues of the deaf. Exceedingly few exchanges of viewpoints manifest a real desire to understand the other person... No one can find a full life without feeling understood at least by one person. Misunderstood, he loses his self-confidence, he loses his faith in life, or even in God.[1]

Listening and giving warm responses are two important skills in dialoguing. There is a technique you can use that will increase your skill in both these areas at the same time. I call it the L & R (Listening and Resonating) method of working with people in predicaments. It is very simple, and very difficult. Simple because of the concept—listen desperately to what the person is saying and with what emotion he is saying it, and then respond with enough of the content and emotion that he feels deeply heard. It is difficult because we often mistake predicaments for problems and we have built a response style of advice-giving and problem-solving.

If a high-school-age boy says to his father, "But, Dad, everyone is going!" the father has many options in responding. One response would be, "OK, name me sixteen." Obviously, this is a dialogue stopper and an argument beginner. An L &

## 47 : LEARNING HOW TO DIALOGUE

R response could be, "I can understand it would be hard to have to tell the guys you can't go." This allows the dialogue to continue. If the father believes he should deny the request, the situation is still better than it would be with the first response, because the *relationship* is better. It is important to know that responding warmly does not mean we are weak. Rather, usually it enables us to maintain standards *and* relationships.

Let's suppose you drive home on a snowy day and you are met by your wife in the living room. She says with a great deal of feeling, "I'm bushed! Do you know what it's like being in a house with three preschool kids all day?" Responses could include (the translations are in parentheses) "It's not much fun being out on those slippery streets, either, you know," (My problem is bigger than your problem); or "Well, my sister has the same situation and it doesn't seem to be a problem for her. Maybe you ought to check with her sometime and see how she manages it," (You're so inefficient!); or "Well, I've been trying to tell you that you just aren't strict enough with them," (You never listen to me!); or "That's too bad: I'm sure tomorrow will be better" (I don't know whether it will be or not, but enough of this talking; let's get supper going!).

An L & R response to "I'm bushed! Do you know what it's like being in a house with three preschool kids all day?" might be, "No, but it sounds like you're really feeling trapped today." This response begins with an honest answer to the question, and then resonates with (echoes) a very deep vibration in the wife's statement. An important guideline for the L & R response is to observe the other person closely for feeling clues, and then to report back in a non-tape-recorder, non-parrot way, this emotion. It *will* seem mechanical and even artificial at first, but that doesn't mean it's phony. It's real, just the same way a new kind of tennis serve or a new golf swing is real, even though at first it's wooden and mechanical. The deeper the habit of advice-giving, the more artificial the L & R approach will seem in the beginning. You will feel it's worth it when you have been able by this method to help a family member emerge from a predicament. However, usually giving warm messages alone is not enough—they need to be straight as well.

## Giving Straight Messages

Someone has called this the stereo generation—we speak out of both sides of our mouth at the same time. However, most people who give bent messages probably don't intend to lie, or even to slant the truth. Rather, as we noticed earlier, a message is bent because it is wrapped around an unspoken, real message. One thinks one thing and says something else. The father who says to his four-year-old son, "Big boys don't cry," gives a bent message. The truth is 1) He is a little boy, and 2) Even big boys (and men) cry sometimes. The disguised message often is, "I'm ashamed of you when you cry." A mother says to her preschool daughter, "Little girls don't fight." This is not a straight message. The truth is, "Little girls do fight sometimes." The unspoken message in this situation is often "Girls who fight when they are little may not turn out to be ladies when they grow up."

One of the best collections of straight messages can be found in the dialogues of Jesus. One time when I was looking for a different kind of Bible study, I settled on this topic. I was amazed to discover the diversity of the people with whom Jesus carried on a dialogue: friends, enemies, little children, Satan, those who needed information, persons needing forgiveness, disciples, Old Testament believers (Moses and Elijah), prostitutes, revolutionaries, poor people, rich

## 49 : LEARNING HOW TO DIALOGUE

people, the powerful, and the powerless, Jews, Gentiles, Samaritans, tax collectors, rabbis, and his heavenly Father. And his messages were straight. When he talked to the Father, in Gethsemane, he told out loud how he felt inside. He told the rich young ruler straight out what he needed to give up to follow him, but he didn't make him do it. After his dialogue at the age of twelve with the teachers in Jerusalem, he gave a straight answer to Mary and Joseph when they came looking for him.

In addition to studying the dialogues of Jesus, one can usually help the straightness of his messages by shortening them. Not all short responses are straight, but they are more likely to be straight than long responses are. I find when I give directions to someone on how to reach a place, my response is likely to be brief and to the point if I know exactly how to get there. It tends to become longer if I am not quite so sure. In the latter case, I may even add, "You can't miss it."

I have done a study, extending over several years, of the length of responses of persons who are training to be counselors. This is rather easily done by tape recording, with the participants' consent, a group discussion, and then analyzing the tape to discover the number of times each person spoke, and the number of seconds he used per response. The number of persons studied now is about 100. Several facts have surfaced. The shortest average response length was three seconds. One can say a ten-word sentence in three seconds. The longest average response was ninety seconds. One can read the Beatitudes aloud in about half that time. A person with an average response length of a minute and a half has an almost insurmountable obstacle in front of him on his path to becoming an effective counselor. The successful counselor must stay with the counselee in his responses. Long responses on the part of the counselor serve to interrupt the train of thought of the counselee.

The average response length of counselors-in-training was found to be twelve to fourteen seconds. One can say several sentences in this length of time. If you do not know how long you tend to talk in discussions, you can find out by timing yourself or asking a friend to time you. This needs to be done over a period of time, and then an average obtained in order to be accurate. If your average response length is more than ten to fifteen seconds, you may wish to work at shortening your responses. Remember that, other things being equal, the shorter your response length, the more you can stay with the other person, and the straighter your messages will be. Still another help in giving effective messages is to make your responses strong.

## Making the Message Strong

The first two helps toward more effective dialogues—warm responses and straight responses—fall in the area of communication skills. Probably most people feel inner warmth toward others; they just need to learn to express that warmth, to warm the person next to them. For most of us, too, it involves shedding some of our insulation. As far as giving straight messages is concerned, if we are honest persons of good will, we need to learn the skill of saying it like it is and then stop talking. But this third area of giving a *strong* message involves much more than skills. It has to do with personal strength. We can't give a strong message if *we* are weak.

Where does personal strength come from? There are a number of references in Scripture which show that one way strength comes to us is through the Lord as we meditate on him and on his Word. Meditation is not just an exercise of the

## 51 : LEARNING HOW TO DIALOGUE

Eastern religions. It is a part of the Hebrew-Christian tradition. As the leadership of the Exodus passed from Moses to Joshua, God told Joshua,

> This book of the law shall not depart out of your mouth, but you shall *meditate* on it day and night, that you may be careful to do according to all that is written in it; for then you shall make your way prosperous, and then you shall have good success. Have I not commanded you? Be strong and of good courage; be not frightened, neither be dismayed; for the Lord your God is with you wherever you go.[2]

In our meditation on the Lord we come to understand that he is with us, and that gives us strength. Also, this passage as well as other Scripture passages simply commands the Christian to *be* strong. Another example is from the New Testament:

> Be watchful, stand firm in your faith, be courageous, be strong.[3]

It appears that we are to make the decision to be strong. Could that mean that when we are weak, it is because we have decided to be weak? At any rate, as we meditate on the Lord, we can choose to be strong because he is with us.

It is important to be strong in a dialogue because the person in a predicament needs to draw strength from others. A very deep predicament for me was the day my mother died. My father had died the year before. In many ways he and I had been closer than my mother and I, so I couldn't figure out why it was harder when my mother died. Lillian told me later that probably it was because she was my last parent. A person can have some of the same feelings of being an orphan in his forties that he would as a child. When the call came, I closed my office door and cried. Later I opened the door, and a few minutes later a friend came in, a sensitive, aware person. He had heard the news. I don't remember that he said anything to me. He just put his hand on my shoulder and voiced a prayer of two or three sentences. He didn't try to do anything *for* me, because he understood he couldn't—he could only be *with* me. And that was what I needed. I felt strength coming to me through his touch and voice. And I'll never forget that warm feeling.

We give scores of messages to others every day. If we work hard to make them warm, and straight, and strong, they can provide caring, truth, and courage to those around us. And they can help people emerge from their predicaments. But it does take work and practice. On the next page are some statements. Write in the response you would make to each one. Make your response as warm, straight, and strong as you can. Use responses that will be likely to continue the dialogue rather than stop it.

## Practice Dialogue Responses

As you fill in the responses below, remember it's not like parachuting—you don't have to be right the first time! There are many ways you could respond that would meet the three guidelines above. After you have written in your responses, compare them to the responses on page 54.

*Situation 1:* Your daughter stomps into the house and says, "I can't stand school another day!"
*Response:*

_____

_____

_____

## 53 : LEARNING HOW TO DIALOGUE

*Situation 2:* Your husband sighs during dinner, and remarks, "Jim Clark had a heart attack this morning. He's better now but it's made me realize this could happen to me."
*Response:*

_____

_____

_____

*Situation 3:* Your wife says to you, "I saw more of you when we were dating than I do now. It seems like you're *always* working late."
*Response:*

_____

_____

_____

*Situation 4:* Your son says, "I heard you and Dad talking last night about moving soon. I don't want to leave here."
*Response:*

_____

_____

_____

*Situation 5:* A friend confides in you, "I've really been down lately. It doesn't seem right for a Christian to get so depressed."
*Response:*

_____

_____

_____

## Responses That Tend to Continue a Dialogue

*Situation 1:* Your daughter stomps in the house and says, "I can't stand school another day!"
*Response:* "It sounds like school has been really hard for you to take today."

*Situation 2:* Your husband sighs during dinner, and remarks, "Jim Clark had a heart attack this morning. He's better now but it's made me realize this could happen to me."
*Response:* "It's made you do some pretty serious thinking about *your own* future?"

*Situation 3:* Your wife says to you, "I saw more of you when we were dating than I do now. It seems like you're *always* working late."
*Response:* It makes me feel good that you want to see more of me. I want to see more of you, too. Let's talk about what can be done about my work obligations."

*Situation 4:* Your son says, "I heard you and Dad talking last night about moving soon. I don't want to leave here."
*Response:* "It would be hard to leave the close friends you have."

*Situation 5:* A friend confides in you, "I've really been down lately. It doesn't seem like it's right for a Christian to get so depressed."
*Response:* "You not only feel discouraged right now, but it's difficult to deal with the guilt feelings, too."

Note that the above responses do not attempt to solve a problem. These are opening responses designed to let the person in the predicament know he is being understood. A plan for action will usually emerge later in the dialogue.

# two: anxiety

*The anxious person propels himself into a fearsome, unreal future by his dread of what is going to happen. What can be done to bring him back into the present?*

# CHAPTER FIVE: ANXIETY-RIDDEN THROUGH PRETENDING

"I want to get rid of this knot in my stomach. There's a tight feeling there nearly all the time. I can't remember anything, and I can't concentrate on what I'm doing." Jane, a 25-year-old slender, tense woman, the mother of a small boy, had just been divorced. She had the characteristic symptoms of anxiety. She moved around in her chair, but couldn't find a comfortable position. One hand tightly clasped the other. Her occasional nervous laughter contradicted her otherwise sad expression. She had difficulty telling her story coherently. It was as if all her blood was being used to meet the needs of her churning stomach and none was left over

## 58 : ANXIETY

for her brain. Her anxiety, although increased by the turmoil of her divorce, had been with her long before she was married.

She remembered when she was in the first grade, her best friend had "dropped" her. She could still feel the hurt of this rejection. "I'll never forget the pain and loneliness I felt. I cried all day." Since that time she had "kept her best foot forward." She felt that just being herself was not quite good enough. In short, she had been pretending for nearly twenty years. The tension in her body was created by a pull in one direction to be herself, and a pull in the other direction to come across to others in some ideal, perfect way. She was now at the breaking point.

Pull a person in opposite directions long enough and hard enough and he'll reach the breaking point—a nervous breakdown. Only he doesn't break in the sense that a cord breaks. Rather, he will choose to escape for awhile until he can rebuild his ability to cope with his predicament.

The anxious person is a person in conflict, one who is pulled two ways. He is tied tightly to a "stretching machine" that he himself has constructed. James puts it this way, "For that person must not suppose that a double-minded man, unstable in all his ways, will receive anything from the Lord."[1] An additional characteristic of the anxious person, then, is instability. How can a person be both rigid and unstable? Imagine a person in a small boat in rough water. He is so frightened that he is "scared stiff" and is "glued" to his seat; being unable to shift his weight from side to side, he thus causes the boat to lack stability. The anxious person begins to lose the ability to adapt.

Charles Dickens talks about anxiety in one section of *Pickwick Papers*.[2] The Pickwickians were spending the Christmas holidays at Manor Farm, and some of them decided

## 59 : ANXIETY-RIDDEN THROUGH PRETENDING

to go skating. Mr. Winkle immediately got himself into a predicament by answering in the affirmative when Wardle asked him, "You skate, of course, Mr. Winkle?" Because he had never skated in his life, and because he lied about it, he began the anxiety-producing process of pretending. He said that, as a matter of fact, he would be very happy to skate, but he had no skates. His friends looked around and found eight pairs of skates available, "Whereat Mr. Winkle expressed exquisite delight, and looked exquisitely uncomfortable." Incidentally, this contradiction of verbal and nonverbal expression is sometimes a sign of anxiety. The words often reflect the image one is trying to produce, and the nonverbal communication shows the real person. Sometimes the nonverbal communication, or body language, may even contradict itself, as when Mr. Winkle quite predictably fell down with a crash while trying to skate: "He was seated on the ice making spasmodic efforts to smile; but anguish was depicted on every lineament of his countenance."

## What Is Anxiety?

Anxiety is "a state of uneasiness and distress about future uncertainties; apprehension; worry."[3] An emotion that is close to anxiety is fear. Fear also impacts on a person with uneasiness and distress. However, there are some important differences between fear and anxiety. Fear has a clear object. A person with a bad cold who is going to give a speech may be afraid that his voice will be rough. On the other hand, if a person has a vague dread every time he speaks that he will be raspy and unclear, that is anxiety. This anxiety, by the way, often brings about sufficient tenseness in the throat that the voice quality is actually lessened.

A college student stops to talk in the hall and says, "I

don't know what to do; I'm afraid my wife is going to leave me." He is right in describing the emotion as fear. The object of his fear—the threat of his wife's leaving—is real, not imagined.

Another example of this fear-anxiety difference is when a person backs off (wisely) from a large, snarling dog; but if he generalizes that fear and cannot stand to be near any dogs, even waggy-tailed, friendly little dogs, then he is in a state of anxiety. In this case it is a specific form of anxiety—phobia.

In addition to having a clear, specific object, fear differs from anxiety in that fear tends to be temporary whereas anxiety is more permanent. As soon as the source of fear is gone, the emotion leaves. Since anxiety has no source that can be pinpointed, it persists. The middle-aged man who waited on me in the hardware store this afternoon confided that it was his first day of work there. He couldn't find the concrete anchors I needed to hold up a shelf, and it was easy to see he was afraid he was doing an inadequate job. Later when we were looking for quarter-inch screws, he couldn't spot them, even though they were on a shelf right in front of him. What first appeared to be fear turned out to be anxiety because it was staying with him and rendering him ineffective even on easy tasks.

Another difference between these two emotions is the extent of the response. A person who is afraid of intruders will lock the doors at night. Another person who is continually anxious about possible intruders and burglars may check the doors many times in the evening to see if they are locked and may lie awake for hours listening to sounds that might suggest someone is trying to enter. The story is told of a man whose wife had always dreaded the thought of burglars. One night she awakened him by whispering in his ear, "There's a noise downstairs." He stumbled out of bed and ran downstairs in time to see a burglar fleeing out a window. He called to the burglar, "Say, would you wait a minute? I'd like my wife to meet you. She's been looking for you for twenty-five years!"

## What Causes Anxiety?

Is anxiety caused by something that happened a long time ago, something we are doing right now, or perhaps some combination of the two? Psychoanalysts believe that anxiety has such strong roots in the past that it is necessary to take the long mental and emotional journey back to childhood. This is why persons who have been psychoanalyzed typically have very good memories. They have used them a great deal. This may also be why some psychiatrists and psychologists are referred to as "headshrinkers" or simply "shrinks"; that is, they help the person regress or "shrink" back to childhood.

Jane's experience (mentioned earlier in this chapter) of being rejected by her best friend when she was in the first grade, shows the early years *are* important in shaping later behavior. However, her recollection of this event and her insights concerning it were insufficient to bring about *present change* in her adult life. A number of psychiatrists and psychologists, including William Glasser and O. Hobart Mowrer,[4] are suggesting that the long trip back to childhood may not be necessary, or even helpful. It is possible that anxiety can be reduced more efficiently by a close look at present behavior rather than a long look at one's personal history. In fact, what seemed to help Jane most in reducing her anxiety was to discuss ways she was presently pretending to be something she was not, and to get a commitment from her regarding ways she would work at being more "real."

## 62 : ANXIETY

Working to change present behavior to reduce anxiety offers a rather rapid way to emerge from the predicament caused by anxiety, as compared to the historical method. I am not suggesting a do-it-yourself approach for persons with advanced anxiety states. Rather I am urging that families use the resources they have to counter anxiety while the involved person is still able to cope successfully.

Is it possible to pinpoint the kinds of present behavior that contribute to the heightening of anxiety? Arthur Jersild has shown that anxiety can result from one's attempt to *act* as his ideal self.[5] This behavior is an attempt to present oneself as he wishes he really were. Jersild gives an example of such behavior:

> For example a person who tries to cope with what he perceives as a predominantly hostile world by being meek, compliant, and self-effacing is bound now and then to feel a surge of revolt against this way of dealing with life. At times he will feel that he is being put upon, that others are taking advantage of his good nature. Instead of always enjoying a virtuous glow of subservience, he will have moments when he feels defiant. He may feel the beginnings of upsurge of rage.[6]

Acting, pretending, "putting one's best foot forward," all short-circuit the arduous process of personality growth. They are attractive, in a day of instant puddings, instant mashed potatoes, and one-minute oatmeal, because they offer fast results. However, like its edible counterparts, the product turns out to be a poor substitute for reality, and the price—anxiety—is too high. In the diagram "The Relationship of Pretending to Anxiety," you can see that the greater the difference between the person we really are and the way we try to come across to others (acting or pretending), the greater the anxiety we will feel.

## 63 : ANXIETY-RIDDEN THROUGH PRETENDING
### THE RELATIONSHIP OF PRETENDING TO ANXIETY

| Real Self—Same as the Self We Show Others | Real Self / Self We Show to Others | Real Self / Self We Show to Others |
|---|---|---|
| No Difference No Anxiety | Small Difference Small Amount of Anxiety | Large Difference Large Amount of Anxiety |

The cause of anxiety that we will be attempting to eliminate or at least reduce, then, is pretending to be what we are not. It may be pretending to forgive, when we still hold a grudge; pretending to love everybody, when we can't stand our next door neighbor; pretending to listen to our five-year-old, when we're busy reading the paper; or telling our children they have to learn to get along with each other, when we haven't yet forgiven our husband or wife for an incident that happened last week.

Joan, a middle-aged woman, had started back to college. She became so anxious that she could no longer concentrate on her studies, and she was considering dropping out of school even though she had good academic ability. As she shared her predicament, her fidgeting increased. She wanted desperately to be a perfect Christian, a perfect mother, a perfect wife, and a perfect student. Her immediate predicament was that her daughter, who was to be married soon, did not want her mother's help in the wedding. But Joan wondered what people would say if she did not assist in the wedding. The more possessive Joan became, the more the distance between the two widened, and the more anxious Joan became. She finally came face-to-face with her pretending when she said, "I've always *said* I wanted my daughter to be independent, but I don't want to let her go."

## How to Recognize Anxiety

Anxiety is a "dis-ease," an uneasiness within oneself. Therefore, the anxious person shows signs of being uncomfortable with himself or with what he is doing. As we have seen, a behavior that produces anxiety is acting, or pretending, instead of just being what we are. Such pretending usually keeps the person on edge because it's false. The pretender always has to keep remembering what role he is playing. He is always afraid that his guard will go down and then he will show his true self. One can keep sweeping the dust under the carpet, but after awhile the lumps begin to show.

This edginess or tenseness often comes out as ambivalent behavior. Ambivalence is one of those indigestible psychological terms referring to the same characteristic as the scriptural term *double-mindedness,* mentioned earlier. It is the interaction of mutually conflicting feelings, thoughts, or goals. When one is ambivalent, he is torn by two opposite feelings or desires.

A young, athletic-looking minister was committed to the virtue of humility. But he found himself thinking back to his days of glory on the football field and track. His name had often been in the sports headlines of the paper. Now he was considering becoming a coach so he could regain some of this recognition he was missing so much. But the ambivalent needs for attention and humility were competing inside him and making him uncomfortable and anxious.

Sometimes a person who has lived with anxiety a long while has learned to cover up some of the most telling signs of ambivalence. Still, the life style may indicate anxiety. Jersild has found that children may reveal anxiety by their life style.

> The one who cannot learn is often an anxious child. The one who will not learn is often an anxious child. The rebel, the cut-up, the scatterbrain, the hostile child, the child who is aggressive and defiant—is often an anxious child. It is not only those who tremble who are anxious.[7]

Paul Barkman has written an excellent commentary on James from the psychoanalytic point of view. In his book *Man in Conflict,* Barkman makes it clear that anxiety is always self-defeating. The anxious person is in a predicament since "he always loses when he wins, because a part of him is on each side of the struggle."[8] This constant failure may bring out more serious needs and behaviors.

The anxious person may begin to believe he is physically ill. He may go from doctor's office to doctor's office with general complaints, seeking treatment or medication. It is important to him that others recognize the authenticity of his illness. The story is told of one man who before his death had this message engraved on his tombstone, "Now will you believe I was sick?" Although the hypochrondriac may be the source of humor for others, he is not a happy person.

## The Effects on the Rest of the Family

An anxiety state in one family member causes confusion in the rest of the family. Remember that pretending is a behavior that causes anxiety. Often the other family members are in a quandary as to what the involved member really wants. This is only natural, since he doesn't know what he wants either. A father may work in family discussions to get across an image of himself as a democratic leader. However, in reality, he may be an authoritarian person who seldom listens to others' ideas. The conflict of a "bossy" life style and an attempted democratic leadership style is anxiety-producing to him and confusing to the rest of the family.

The anxious family member often causes frustration among other family members. They try to help but usually only make matters worse. Because of the bent messages he is giving (saying two opposite things at the same time), they don't know how to respond to him in a helping way or, in fact, how to respond to him at all. If a mother complains that she is lonely because she is stuck at home with three preschool children and never gets a chance to get out and make friends, the family may try to help her. However, if she is staying home because she is too frightened to reach out to other people since they might reject her, then those family members who are trying to help her will rapidly become frustrated.

Anxiety in one person usually causes disruption in the entire family. The anxious person is in pain, and usually in a family when one person is hurting, the entire family is hurting. A thirteen-year-old eighth grader had a severe reading problem. He did the best he could, but adults were often saying to him, "You could do better if you would just try harder" (which, translated, means, "You're lazy!"). During this particular semester he had more reading to do than ever. The end of the grading period was approaching and he was sure that his grades in several subjects would be lower than

## 67 : ANXIETY-RIDDEN THROUGH PRETENDING

he had ever received. When his parents asked him how things were going, he said, "Oh, all right, I guess," or shook the question off in another way. But he knew the time was coming when there would be a confrontation, and the pretension that things were all right was making him more anxious by the day. He was edgy and hard to live with. He became angry when his brother asked if he could borrow his bike. He snapped at his sister, and sulked when his parents told him to do something. The whole family was upset.

It may be seen that because of the devastating effects of anxiety, the anxious person needs to learn how to reduce his anxiety before the downward spiral reaches whirlpool dimensions.

### Questions
1. Is there an area of your life where you are afraid to come across "real" to others?
2. What would be the worst thing that would happen if you stopped pretending in that area and let your imperfect self show?
3. At what times of the day do you feel the most tense? What activities are you involved in when the tension is the highest?

# CHAPTER SIX: HUMILITY: AN AID IN REDUCING ANXIETY

Lucille was a middle-aged, hard-working, competent elementary school teacher. She was courageous in her Christian witness and led a weekly Bible study attended by some of her fellow faculty members. One day during a coffee break in the teachers' lounge, another teacher said to her, "Your birthday's next Thursday; several of us would like to take you out to dinner that evening. How about it?" Immediately Lucille felt both happy and miserable—happy because her colleagues wanted to do something special for her, and miserable because her dentures sometimes slipped and clicked when she was eating salads!

## 69 : HUMILITY: AN AID IN REDUCING ANXIETY

She was far from satisfied with her reply, "Well—ah—next week's going to be a busy one for me, so I guess I'd better not, but thanks anyway." She knew she was not coming across straight, and she feared her friends would think she didn't appreciate their thoughtfulness. Later she realized that her pride had kept her from sharing the truth. Is it possible that pride often keeps us from sharing our weaknesses? Sometimes it may even keep us from seeking help.

What can the anxious person do to help himself? If he is very anxious and if he is not viewing situations realistically at all, he should seek professional help. As a matter of fact, however, many Christians are opposed to seeking counseling help. At the center of this opposition is often the feeling, "I'm ashamed to admit as a Christian that I have personal problems and that I need help with them. It is a discredit to the Lord and to me." Actually, it is a mark of maturity to seek help when we need it. About two of three Christians who come to me for counseling begin by saying directly or indirectly, "I'm a Christian and I shouldn't be having these kinds of problems." I usually reply with something like, "Oh, did you resign from the human race when you became a Christian?" Then we laugh and begin to work.

Trying to see a situation as it really is presents a problem of awareness, because each of us *thinks* he is viewing the situation realistically. We are prisoners of our own perception. To escape this homemade prison, we need to open ourselves to the perceptions of others *concerning us.* I work in a college and, since colleges run on committees, I spend quite a number of hours each week in committee. (In fact, I've said to Lillian that I hope I don't die in committee, as some resolutions and plans do.) Sometime ago I began to be aware that I was upset each week after one particular committee meeting. As nearly as I could pinpoint my feeling, I was mad!

Finally, I shared where I was with a close friend who also served on that committee. He told me he was aware of my upset condition and that he had observed me becoming slightly impatient, then quite impatient, then irritated, then angry. Together we worked out a plan. At the first twinge of impatience, I would speak up as soon as the conversational traffic permitted, and talk about what was happening in the committee process that made me impatient. The result of this plan was that the committee functioned a bit more effectively, and I left the meeting relaxed. But until I opened up myself to feedback (an honest statement from another person concerning me), I was unable to rid myself of the bad feelings.

## The Feeling of Anxiety

In the last decade we have become keenly aware of outer space, objects millions of miles away. However, we are usually only dimly aware of "inner space," the body parts and movements just inside our own skins. We need to develop a sensitivity to this inner space. The flow of adrenalin, the quivering in the stomach, the dryness of the throat, the clenching of the fist, and moistness of the eyes are important clues to our feeling states. In order to observe or monitor our own anxiety, it is especially important to become aware of parts of the body working against each other. For example, if we open our mouth as if to talk, and at the same time put our hand to our mouth as if to shut the speech off, we may be feeling anxious about what we plan to say. The "reluctant" or "hesitant" walk may also provide clues to our emotions. A forced smile provides evidence of inner conflict.

The primary guideline we need to remember in recognizing the beginning of anxiety is to ask ourselves, "What is

## 71 : HUMILITY: AN AID IN REDUCING ANXIETY

happening in my body?" If we become aware of the little nudges our body occasionally gives us, it may not be necessary for our body to give us large jolts, such as migraine headaches or peptic ulcers (although it should be noted that not all migraine headaches or ulcers are traceable to anxiety).

## The Feeling of Peace

Anxiety is less difficult to prevent than to reduce or eliminate—but that doesn't mean it's easy. One way to get a bearing on anxiety is to try to answer the question, "What is the opposite feeling from anxiety?"

Recently at a renewal conference, a woman about thirty got up to share some of her feelings and experiences. Although she didn't discuss the anxiety that was gripping her, she showed in many different ways she was in a very anxious state. She was so anxious, in fact, that she didn't stop talking. She just kept explaining and then explained the explanations. The host pastor rose to his feet at one point when she stopped for breath, and asked another pastor to go up and stand with her and pray that she might receive the gift of peace. The other pastor put his arm around her and asked that God would give her peace. She left the microphone in a calm and relaxed state.

The host pastor's insight—that an anxious person needs peace—was both obvious and rare. If peace, then, is the opposite of anxiety, how do we gain peace? In some situations, as in the one above, it is received from God as a gift. However, there are Scripture references that indicate we have some responsibility in building a Christian life style that makes peace possible.

The example of the Lord—the Prince of Peace—is instructive. He was humble, open, responsive, relaxed, and straightforward. By contrast, the Pharisees were proud, closed, cold, uptight, and devious. The Pharisees were concerned about appearances, Jesus was concerned about truth; the Pharisees focused on projecting an image, Jesus focused on reality; in short, while the Pharisees were pretending to be what they were not, Jesus was simply being himself.

If Jesus himself chose the way of humility, then it seems reasonable that in our own quest for peace we will need to choose the same way. What does this mean in our everyday lives? It means making a commitment to be real, rather than to act like the ideal self that we would like others to see in us. It means admitting it when we are wrong. Above all, it means no pretending—none. It means some long dialogues with others close to us so we can get a better look about whether we come across "whole." Carl Rogers has said that the reason everyone loves babies is that they come across whole. If they are hungry, they feel it in their stomachs, they are aware of it in their heads, and they say it (in the only way they know) with their mouths. The incongruent, or splintered, person may feel anger in his stomach, deny it in his head, and communicate a mixed message of sweetness and sarcasm.

## Humility—A Resource in the Move Away from Anxiety

How can we use humility as a weapon in our battle against anxiety? According to the dictionary, the attitude of humility "stresses lack of pride, pretense, or assertiveness."[1] The word "pretense" grabs our attention inasmuch as we have seen that pretending is a behavior that causes our anxiety to rocket. So—how do we stop pretending? The dictionary definition suggests that as we increase in humility, we decrease in pretense.

## 73 : HUMILITY: AN AID IN REDUCING ANXIETY

The Bible encourages the *cultivation* of humility (attempts at instant humility often come across as phony) and its companion personality characteristics—meekness and lowliness. Meekness is similar to humility and carries the added idea of the absence of wrath and vindictiveness. Meekness is not a trait that is usually sought after, partly because it is often misunderstood. A bit of grafitti in the newspaper put it this way, "If the meek really do inherit the earth, they won't be able to keep it very long." The implication is that the meek person lacks strength. The truth of the matter is that it is only the meek person who is strong. The tyrant may act strong, as Khrushchev did when he once banged his shoe on the table during a meeting, but a strong person does not have to resort to attention-getting techniques. Moses was referred to as "very meek, more than all men that were on the face of the earth,"[2] and he was able to stand before a tyrant and say, "Let my people go." The subsequent adventures of Moses show he was not lacking in courage. Jesus referred to himself as "meek and lowly in heart," but he often demonstrated his strength by standing alone for the truth. The meek person, then, is strong, but does not seek revenge. Lowly, according to Webster, "is close to humble, and may stress lack of pretentiousness."[3]

Humility is defined in terms of negatives. Does that mean it is a negative concept? Not really. Humility is like a clean plate glass window in the front of a store. People can see the merchandise as it is. Humility is also like a true mirror that lets us see ourselves as we are. Pride and pretending are like the "crazy mirrors" in the sideshow of a carnival, in which we and others with us see distorted images of ourselves.

The classic passage in the Bible on humility is Philippians, Chapter 2. The Apostle Paul commented on the kind of life Jesus lived, and urged Christians to have the mind of

Christ. "Do nothing from selfishness or conceit, but in humility count others better than yourselves. Let each of you look not only to his own interests, but also to the interests of others" (Philippians 2:3, 4). The two personality characteristics encouraged here are humility (not pretending to be more than we are), and altruism (being concerned for others). The apostle then delineates how the life of Jesus gives us an example of these two crucial personality traits. Jesus humbled himself step-by-step, first by putting aside his godly prerogatives, and finally by accepting death on a cross. The companion trait of altruism was present since he took these radical steps out of his concern for others' welfare.

## Ways to Detect and Deal with Anxiety-Producing Behaviors

Not all anxiety is caused by pretending. Therefore, we may need to look for other causes. But for the time being, let's assume that in some part of our life we are being pretentious. We need not go back into our past looking for some incident that started it all. We can rather expect that we can find sufficient clues in our present behavior. Once we start pretending in some part of our lives, this behavior goes on daily. Usually our anxiety reaches its highest peak at the time we are pretending. Our investigation can become like the game of finding the button, in which the onlookers say, "You're getting hotter," or "You're getting cold." Our own body reactions will lead us to the present behavior that is fueling the anxiety.

Jan, a married woman in her twenties was feeling anxiety but was not aware of any actions on her part that were making her anxious. She knew her predicament involved her relationship with her husband. "He always wants to work

## 75 : HUMILITY: AN AID IN REDUCING ANXIETY

more hours and make more money. I'd rather have him home than have the extra money he makes." Jan was given the task by a counselor of writing "Twelve Things I Love to Do."[4] (Instructions for working through this insight-producing exercise are given on pages 79-82.) Among the questions asked by the counselor was "How many of the twelve things you love to do require money?" She was surprised when she saw that nearly all the activities she loved required money. In a flash of insight she said, "No wonder he's working all the time; he has to, just to support me!" She then began to work very hard to move to a simpler life style, and one that required much less money. A letter several months later told how they were spending much more time together—and how they were learning to enjoy each other. The point of this example is that although she was unable to pinpoint the exact source of her anxiety, she was aware of the general area of upset.

It is important simply to listen to those around you. They may say things like, "Why didn't you tell him you didn't know how to do it?" or "Are we doing this just because people expect us to?" Families have a way of easing the air out of stuffed shirts. We get back down to natural size much faster, however, if we are nondefensive, and give thoughtful, honest answers to questions like these.

Once we have detected the presence and the cause of the anxiety, the most effective way of dealing with it is to talk to someone to whom we pretended, or in whose presence we did so. This amounts to confession, which is a way of healing. "Therefore confess your sins to one another, and pray for one another, that you may be healed" (James 5:16a). Dr. Hobart Mowrer tells the story of a mother, a patient in a mental hospital, who had battered her baby daughter and almost choked her to death. The mother wrote,

> These incidents, in themselves, are bad enough. But perhaps even worse, I'd been pretending all this time to be a "good" person. I put on such a good front that no one knew any different. Our immediate families suspected something was wrong, but they had no idea what my problems were.[5]

Then she relates how she confessed first to her husband, then to her parents, and then to some very close friends what she had done. After she had dropped her pretense of being a "good mother" she began to move toward mental health.

> Everything seemed different. Even the colors of the outside world looked sharper and more beautiful... I had a new life just waiting to be filled with something other than deceit and pretense.[6]

Mowrer makes the point that a confession to a professional person alone, such as a psychologist, psychiatrist, or minister, would not have been enough. She was relieved from the anxiety and guilt by letting those she lived with see her as she was. This move to being genuine and honest is a move toward wholeness.

The feelings and behaviors that accompany anxiety, and the growth in humility and openness that are necessary to reduce it, are illustrated in detail in the experiences of a man I'll call Jerry. He is a gentle, compassionate man whom I grew to respect a great deal.

## The Case of Jerry

Jerry, a middle-aged Christian man, was referred by his pastor for counseling. Jerry presented two problems during the first session—he became depressed very easily, and he was unable to talk with his wife when he became angry with her. He showed by his agitated body movements and

## 77 : HUMILITY: AN AID IN REDUCING ANXIETY

by his somewhat breathless speech that he was feeling a great deal of anxiety.

I recently asked Jerry if he would like to share with others his experience in moving toward peace. He said he would, and following are excerpts of his story as he told it:

> I grew up as a boy in a family that didn't really show a lot of love toward one another, and even between my mother and father, and yet there was love ... but we really never showed love to one another through kisses or hugs or that type of showing our emotions. I'm sure my parents didn't communicate, at least like they should have, and this carried over into my own married life.
>
> I had some strong points, but you know all I could think of was my weak points, the places where I had failed, and just simply hadn't functioned like I should—The things I had done wrong kept bouncing up in my life and more and more I began to feel like I was a failure because I was reminded so much of the things I had failed in rather than my good points....
>
> For a long time I was very conscious of my own weaknesses and if anybody criticized me I would immediately clam up and in fact my mind would probably go blank. Everything quit. I mean, I couldn't laugh about it; it was just simply like I was being shot at—might be one way of explaining it.
>
> There was a time when I was at my lowest that I just wanted to get away—to escape. When I got in my car and drove to work, I just wanted to keep on driving. I thought about going to a mental hospital and turning myself in.
>
> I felt like—another way of describing it—like a twig out in the middle of a stream just caught in the stream and absolutely helpless.
>
> I was always tired and yet there was no real physical reason. I just simply could not keep up with the conversations or what was going on around

> me because I was so wrapped up in my own feelings and emotions and problems and it was very difficult for me to remember ... and I wasn't awake enough to anticipate and be prepared for what was going to happen....

Jerry captured very well the feelings of an anxious person. He expressed the trapped feelings—the need to escape. He shared the tiredness which inner conflict always produces. He explained how he had allowed criticism to immobilize him. When he got upset with himself or his work or his wife, he closed himself off from others by not talking to them. Naturally this mystified and irritated his wife, and decreased the fellowship they had together. His anger at himself and his wife, coupled with his failure feelings in other areas, contributed further to his anxiety.

> Especially at the beginning of my recovery, or when I began to find out the reasons for my problem, many times I had to *force* myself to say what I wanted to say ... I was trying to change something I had been doing for years and my mind was in a rut, and I just couldn't overcome it overnight; one can expect to slip back in defeat sometimes....
>
> My progress has been slow and erratic at times and discouraging, but I've learned not to dwell so much on the discouragements. I look more now for ways to correct what isn't going well and to focus on the positive side of life....
>
> Uh—probably one of the things now as far as getting along in life ... I'm not bashful about sharing my experiences in the past. I don't flash them on billboards but if there is a reason to do so, I share some of my experiences.
>
> The improvement of my relationship with my wife has been slow, and like I mentioned before it's hard to get out of that rut.... There are times yet when I find it difficult to share just the way I feel, but every

# HUMILITY: AN AID IN REDUCING ANXIETY

time I share, I gain confidence in myself and confidence in my wife that she still loves me and pretty much accepts me the way I am....

As far as my outlook on life, the thing that stabilizes a person is God's word, "Thou wilt keep him in perfect peace whose mind is stayed on thee, for he trusteth in thee." So in the first place it takes effort, and in the second place we have to learn to trust God....

Jerry's recovery began when he forced himself to share his feelings and confess his discouragement and anger to his wife, whether he felt like it or not. When he got these feelings out, rather than simmer with resentment and anger, he felt more respect for himself and more love for his wife.

He now sees himself as having more growth to make, but also as having made considerable growth. He has better communication with his wife and shows a more loving attitude toward her. He is more productive in his work. He meets Freud's definition of mental health, "A person is mentally healthy if he loves well and works well."

A common element in Jan's and Jerry's move toward wholeness was their growth in awareness regarding their present behaviors. You may want to work through the same exercise that Jan worked through, in order to discover more about your present behaviors and the meaning they have for you.

## Twelve Things I Love to Do

Think of twelve things you really love to do and write them in the space provided on the next page. Do all your writing to the right of the numbers. Just write them down in any way they come to your mind. They do not need to be rank-ordered. Think of activities that really excite you. Write

## 80 : ANXIETY

in these things now. To learn the most from your work, do not turn the page for further instructions until you have completed writing all twelve.

TWELVE THINGS I LOVE TO DO

1. _____
2. _____
3. _____
4. _____
5. _____
6. _____
7. _____
8. _____
9. _____
10. _____
11. _____
12. _____

1. I learned that I _____
   _____

2. I learned that I _____
   _____

3. I learned that I _____
   _____

## 81 : HUMILITY: AN AID IN REDUCING ANXIETY

Now place coding marks to the left of the numbers of the twelve things you love to do.

1. Place a $ to the left of the number of each of the twelve things you love to do that requires money—let's say $2.00 or more. Eating in a restaurant would be an activity that would be marked with a $. Going to Sunday school would not. Walking in the rain would not.
2. Place an M to the left of each of the things you love to do that your mother loves or loved to do. Do the same with an F for father, and an S for your spouse.
3. Place a PD in front of each of the things you love to do that your parents would disapprove of or would have disapproved of.
4. Place an S before a spiritual growth activity such as prayer or Bible study.
5. Place a CH before any activity that involves your church.
6. Place an H before any activity in which you help others.
7. Place an R before any activity that involves risk-taking, that is, it is either physically or psychologically dangerous.
8. Place a CR before any activity that requires creativity, for example, writing a poem or painting a picture.
9. Place an A in front of any thing you love to do that you typically do alone.
10. Write Fam to the left of any of the things you love to do that you usually do with your family.
11. Write PS to the left of any of the things you love to do that require physical skills or physical strength.
12. Write R to the left of any activity that involves reading.
13. Write 5 in front of any activity that you loved to do five years ago.
14. Write 65 in front of any activity that you will love to do at retirement. A common question here is, "But will I be able to?" The answer is usually, "Yes."
15. To find out how up to date you are on your values, write D in front of any you have done today, W to the

## 82 : ANXIETY

left of those you have done in the last week but not the last day, M on those you have done in the last month but not in the last week, and Y on those you've done in the last year but not in the last month.

Now you are ready for the last step in this value clarification exercise. Go through the coding marks and look for patterns. For example, how many of the things you love to do, do you do alone? How many involve your family, your church? How many values do you share with your husband or wife? After you have found several patterns, finish the "I learned's" at the bottom of the page. These are three things you learned about yourself by working through this exercise—three areas of your personality and value system you have become more aware of.

# CHAPTER SEVEN: JUST AS YOU ARE

Judging from the toys on the shelf which the young couple were looking at, I decided they were shopping for about a two- or three-year-old. It was Christmas time, and I was selling in the toy department of a store in Kansas City, attempting to supplement my teaching income. The couple had their backs to me as I approached them, and both of them were looking at a toy truck on the shelf as I asked, "May I help you?" I wasn't really prepared for the response, because there was none. They didn't turn around, say, "No, thanks," or "We're just looking," or anything. As I walked back across the department to resume putting a tricycle together, I found myself judging them, and saying little sentences in my head, like "I was friendly to them; so why did they ignore me? It wouldn't have taken much effort for them to have been courteous. They didn't even turn around to look at me. I don't think they cared whether I was there or not." I looked up a minute or two later from the direction sheet of the tricycle, and noticed the couple were facing each other. Then they put their hands out in front of them—and began communicating in sign language! They hadn't heard a word I'd said. As I looked back down at the direction sheet, I could feel my face getting red. I had made a judgment before all the evidence was in. When I got home that night, I thought, I wonder if I've made a *habit* of judging people before all the evidence is in. I wonder if the evidence is *ever* all in?

## Be Accepting

I learned something that Christmas in the toy department—that it's necessary to suspend my own judgment and to accept people just as they are, if I want to help them. This approach seems to work in helping an anxious family member. If a person is causing or increasing his anxiety by pretending, then those around him need to help him feel safe in just being himself. When a person is accepted just as he is, his need to pretend begins to wither. Carl Rogers put it in a thought-provoking way, "People are just as wonderful as sunsets if I can let them be. I don't try to control a sunset. I watch it with awe as it unfolds, and I like myself best when appreciating the unfolding of a life."[1]

The paradox is that when people are accepted as they are, they begin to want to change! The New Testament is full of this strange action-reaction sequence. Jesus chose to go to Zacchaeus's house as a guest, rather than denouncing him for his greed as a chief tax collector. Many Christians would criticize Jesus for this action (if it had been anyone else but Jesus) by saying something like, "I don't know about that; it looks to me like going to his house would just show him and others that you approve of what he has been doing." But Zacchaeus's response? "Behold, Lord, the half of my goods I give to the poor; and if I have defrauded anyone of anything, I restore it fourfold."[2] Could it be that when we are willing to come close to people and to be with them just as they are, they begin to feel an inside pressure to change, much stronger than any pressure we could place on them?

To accept another person is to love him—anxiety and all. Robert R. Carkhuff, who has spent much of his life researching the most effective ways of helping, has suggested an important step in acceptance:

> Next, it is important to suspend our judgment in listening, at least initially. If we are going to listen to what the helpee has to say, *we must suspend temporarily the things which we say to ourselves.* Just let the helpee's message sink in without trying to make decisions about it.[3]

I saw again the necessity of family members accepting each other when I observed a young woman who was working very hard at reconciliation with her husband. She felt they could make it together "if he would just share his feelings with me. Most of the time I just don't know where he is." As she continued to talk about their life together, she remembered he used to cry at times but when he did, "I lost respect for him. I can't stand to see a man cry." She then began to realize that he *had* shared feelings with her, very deep feelings, but that her nonacceptance of these feelings had caused him to begin concealing his emotions from her. As she dealt with her own predicament, she began to help her husband deal with his.

In addition to suspending our judgment of an anxious family member, there are several other guidelines that sometimes work in helping. I say, "sometimes," because no guideline seems to work all the time and there are times when none seem to work.

## Be Empathetic

One of the most researched helping characteristics is empathy. It is also one of the characteristics most difficult to define. One way to approach a definition is to look at what empathy is not. An opposite characteristic of empathy is to make a "big deal" of it when we are trying to help somebody. Too many persons use the "foreign aid" approach in extending help to another family member: "I don't have any problems, and you have a problem; I'm going to do something for you." This condescending approach usually causes the other person to back off. When we use this approach we are treating the other family member as an object rather than a person.

The best way we can help a person who is immersed in the predicament of anxiety is to do something *with* him rather than *for* him. The importance of "withness" can be illustrated in our feelings. Empathy is feeling with a person; sympathy is feeling sorry for a person. In the first emotion there is a relationship; in the second there is isolation. If we feel sorry for our daughter who is very anxious at the moment, we thereby add one more burden to her load of anxiety. If we feel with her and realize we have felt some of the conflicts and tearing she feels, the interpersonal relationship is strengthened, and the anxiety may be lessened.

Empathy, of course, did not come into existence in the last quarter of the twentieth century. When God set about resolving the human predicament, he didn't reach down from

# 87 : JUST AS YOU ARE

heaven to straighten us out, but rather he *came* down to be with us: "For because he himself has suffered and been tempted, he is able to help those who are tempted."[4] The lesson that Jesus taught here is a simple one that can change our entire way of helping: In the deepest kind of predicaments we cannot do something *for* a person until we are involved *with* him.

## Invest Time

An obvious, and often overlooked, way of getting involved with an anxious family member is to invest our time in that person. I remember a gracious, dedicated Christian man who sought counseling help for his thirteen-year-old boy. As he told his story, he said he wished he had more time to spend with his boy, but his business was expanding and he had almost no time for this relationship. I remember he was shocked and hurt when I said I would not begin a counseling relationship with his boy. I explained that his boy was anxious because he was trying to become a man, and the future looked shaky to him because of the predicaments he found himself in. He needed to spend time with his father in order to emerge from these predicaments.

The most effective way of discovering how much time we are spending with family members is to keep a time chart for a week, such as the "Time Investment Chart" shown here. Record only the time you spend with each family member in a one-to-one situation. This is not to say that the time you spend with your total family, or two or three of them together, is not important. That time is very important. Rather, the idea behind the time chart is to record an often overlooked measure of time investment—the time invested in family members one at a time. If you will keep this chart carefully, you will be surprised at the results.

| FAMILY MEMBER | NUMBER OF MINUTES I SPENT WITH EACH FAMILY MEMBER DAILY THIS WEEK ||||||| TOTAL MINUTES FOR THE WEEK |
|---|---|---|---|---|---|---|---|---|
| | Sun | Mon | Tues | Wed | Thurs | Fri | Sat | |
| Spouse | | | | | | | | |
| Oldest Child | | | | | | | | |
| Middle Child | | | | | | | | |
| Youngest Child | | | | | | | | |
| (Add to chart if needed) | | | | | | | | |

One of the concepts behind time investment is nourishment. Look at the chart for *patterns* when you have completed it. (Be sure to record daily.) Is there one child for whom you have more than one "0" recorded for the week? If this is a pattern for other weeks as well, this particular child may become "malnourished" emotionally. Every person needs what has been called "human nourishment" to grow psychologically. Another word for human nourishment is love, if love is defined accurately as some act of caring that *comes across* from one person to another. If it is just an uncommunicated glow or feeling we have about someone, it doesn't help that person. Nourishment is a term that shows that something comes across in a growth-producing way from one person to another.

Nourishment is a word that describes the effect of the time Jesus invested in his "family"—the Twelve. Time investment was one of his stated purposes in forming this group. "And he appointed twelve, *to be with him*, and to be sent out to preach and have authority to cast out demons."[5] And Jesus *was* with them. He spent time with them as a group and individually. He corrected them, praised them, dialogued with them, and in many other ways, he nourished them. Always, he invested large amounts of time with them.

Some ask, "It doesn't matter, does it, if I spend only a small amount of time with my child, as long as the quality of that time is good?" My answer is, "Yes, it matters a great deal to your child." Some have said, "Well, isn't it better to spend a little good time with your child than a lot of angry, or bad time?" Of course, but that's not really the point. The point is that children need chunks of time investment. We cannot expect our children to develop well on very small amounts of food, no matter how nutritious these small bits are. A diet of

## 90 : ANXIETY

vitamin pills only would be hard to take!

How much time should we spend with another member of the family? By asking that question we show that we are in a predicament. Another question might be, "How much time do I *want* to spend with him?" This second question puts the issue in terms of love rather than duty. When couples come for counseling, I require them to spend some "prime time" with each other every day, a time when they are at their best mentally, physically, and emotionally.[6] This usually turns out to be one of the most difficult requirements of the counseling relationship. Many couples whose marriages are shaky have been spending almost no prime time with each other. As we negotiate for the amount of prime time they will spend with the other person daily, I begin by suggesting an hour. Often the couple begins by agreeing with each other. "We don't have *any* prime time we can spend with each other"—often this is the first issue they have agreed on for some time! But I don't buy it. We may settle on a half-hour, or in some cases, fifteen minutes. Now the point is they usually can make the time but they don't want to spend it with each other—or at least one of the two doesn't want to spend it with the other. Often one person, usually the wife, says, "Why, I saw more of him before we were married than I do now." But now they have become abrasive to each other and the time together is not pleasant.

To answer the question, "How much time should I spend with...?" you might wish to see if you are spending a minimum of fifteen minutes daily with each member of the family in a one-to-one relationship. Is it possible to build and maintain a relationship on less than this? Then in a month do another time chart. Often persons who begin in this way find they are soon spending more time with family members because it is fun. I remember one couple who finally agreed to

# 91 : JUST AS YOU ARE

spend fifteen minutes a day prime time with each other. They reported after one month they often spend an hour or two a day with each other because "the time just seemed to get away," when they were together—just like the old dating days when 11:00 P.M. or midnight came so fast.

## Use Eye Contact

In Thornton Wilder's play *Our Town*, Emily chooses to relive her twelfth birthday, after she had died at the age of twenty-six. She tries, over breakfast, to get Mrs. Webb, her mother, to look at her. But Mrs. Webb seems to be more concerned about the tasks at hand than the persons in the room.

Finally, Emily in her sadness and frustration calls all human beings blind people. She labeled human beings as blind because they didn't really see her. They made her breakfast and gave her gifts, but they didn't look at her.

There are some poems, plays, and novels that I reread every few years because they speak to me about the way I need to live. *Our Town* is one of these. It reminds me to take time to look at my wife and children, my friends, and strangers.

The use of eye contact helps us to see the other members of our family "just as they are"—happy, sad, eager, or anxious. The anxious person desperately needs other people to be aware of him. He senses that awareness when people look at him in a way that says some of the following: "I see you," "I recognize your presence," "I'm glad you're here," "I'm not afraid of you," and mostly, "I'm *with* you."

A pleasant, worried mother of two children came to talk about Don, her junior-high-age boy. He had gotten into so many predicaments at home and school that she knew something had to be done. The thing she wanted to do was to build a relationship with him. She said Don was willing to talk some with her but they usually didn't talk very long, or about things that really mattered. As she described the way she talked, she discovered she rarely used eye contact in her conversations with him. She nearly always looked at some task, such as the dishes she was washing or the clothes she was folding. As a result Don didn't feel she was really with him. Through a series of task assignments which required her to look at him when they talked together, she began gradually to increase the length and quality of their conversations.

With very anxious persons, particularly if they are depressed, it is difficult to make eye contact because they are usually looking down or away. It is necessary to try other ways to help such a person.

## Get in Touch

There are some understandings and skills that are helpful in working with the extremely anxious, panicky person. The panicked person is concerned about survival and therefore is future-oriented. It is not possible to reason with him in his panicked state, because he is not in the realistic present—he is in the unrealistic, threatening future. Also, he is like a broken record. He is usually down to one option—he sees only one way out.

You have to help this very anxious family member move from the *future* to the *present* to get him from the "panic button" to the "hold button." Use eye contact if he will look at you. Also, use touch. Put your hand on his shoulder, hug him, give him a neck or back rub, take his hand, or in some other way that he will accept get in touch with him. This will help pull him back into the present. It is rather unnatural and awkward to do any of these things if your relationship to your child has been an antiseptic (nontouching) one previously. Yet, even if this is the case, it is still worth trying.

Touching seemed to come naturally to Jesus. He touched people wherever he went. He touched a leper, a blind man, the casket of a dead man, and he held little children. He let people touch him—a strange assortment of people, a sick woman, John, who was one of the "Sons of Thunder," who sometimes leaned against him at the table, and a woman of questionable reputation, whom he allowed to wash his feet with her tears, dry them with her hair, and then anoint them. It didn't look right to the Pharisees. This touching business made them uncomfortable. One of them said to himself, "If this man were a prophet, he would have known who and what sort of woman this is who is touching him, for she is a sinner."[7] Jesus turned toward the woman and said to Simon,

> Do you see this woman? (As Emily said, "We don't take time to look at one another.") I entered your house, you gave me no water for my feet, but she has wet my feet with her tears and wiped them with her hair. You gave me no kiss, but from the time I came in she has not ceased to kiss my feet. You did not anoint my head with oil, but she has anointed my feet with ointment. Therefore, I tell you, her sins, which are many, are forgiven, for she loved much; but he who is forgiven little loves little.[8]

And he said to her, "Your sins are forgiven." Jesus allowed this sinful, anxious woman to touch him. And she drew strength and wholeness from that experience of touching.

Sometimes touching isn't enough to calm a very panicky person, and to draw them out of their dread of the future. You can also utilize *activities* to help bring the person back to the present. Len, an aware, intelligent man about forty, was startled to learn that his boy was planning to run away with the boy's best friend. This friend was in an almost intolerable situation at home and didn't feel he could confide in either of his parents. Len figured out that it was the loyalty of his own son that made him want to go along with the panicked boy. Also, Len knew this other boy needed a weekend away from home so he could think better. Therefore, Len got permission from the other set of parents and took both boys away for a weekend fishing trip. In this ingenious way, he legitimized the runaway experience, got the involved boy out of his panicked state, allowed his own boy to remain loyal to his friend, and provided both of them with an adult supervisor for their weekend "runaway." He also got in a lot of talking time with both of them over the weekend.

Once you get a person "on hold," then you can usually have a conversation with him. It is important that you encourage him to talk about his fears. Don't try to give him answers, especially early in the conversation. He's heard these before and they haven't made sense to him, or he would have used them. After he has fully explored his fears, then you can encourage him to come up with alternatives. Help him examine the consequences of these alternatives. The main thing is to let him know you are *with* him. It is this understanding, more than anything else, that will keep him from pressing the panic button again.

## Questions

1. The following guidelines were given for helping the anxious person:

| | | | | | | | | | | |
|---|---|---|---|---|---|---|---|---|---|---|
| Be Accepting | 1 | 2 | 3 | 4 | 5 | 6 | 7 | 8 | 9 | 10 |
| Be Empathic | 1 | 2 | 3 | 4 | 5 | 6 | 7 | 8 | 9 | 10 |
| Invest Time | 1 | 2 | 3 | 4 | 5 | 6 | 7 | 8 | 9 | 10 |
| Use Eye Contact | 1 | 2 | 3 | 4 | 5 | 6 | 7 | 8 | 9 | 10 |
| Get in Touch | 1 | 2 | 3 | 4 | 5 | 6 | 7 | 8 | 9 | 10 |

## 95 : JUST AS YOU ARE

On the above scale to the right of the guideline, circle the number that accurately describes your amount of skill in this area, with 1 being none of the quality, and 10 being a great deal of that quality. For example, if you are accepting some of the time, but frequently find yourself judging others, you might circle 4 or 5.

2. Of those skills which you rated lowest, which one would you be willing to commit yourself to improve?

# three: hurt and anger

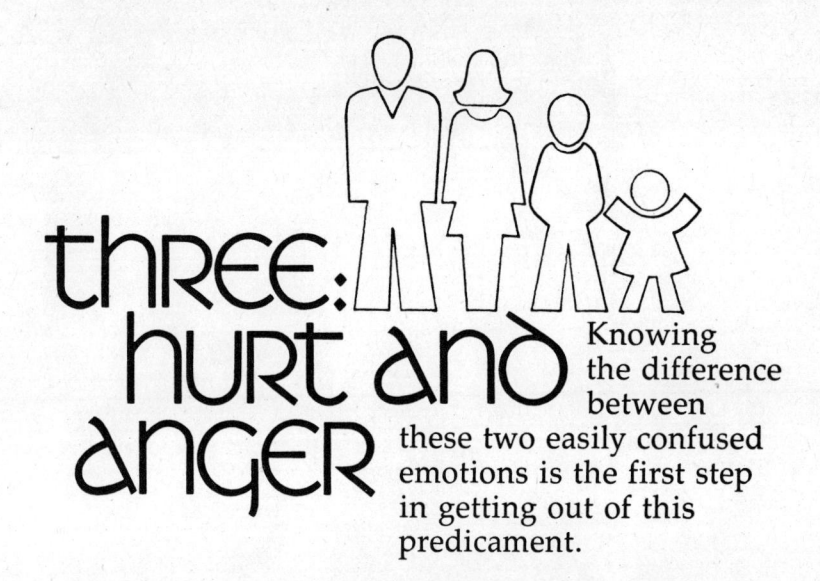

Knowing the difference between these two easily confused emotions is the first step in getting out of this predicament.

## CHAPTER EIGHT: HURT AND ANGER— KNOWING THE DIFFERENCE

As the young couple entered my office, I was struck by two first impressions—they were a handsome looking pair, but they looked so very sad. Bill, a slender, dark-haired man, carried himself erect with a rather determined look on his face. Jo Ann, a tall, blonde woman about the same age as her husband, looked scared and had a reluctant walk rather than her husband's marching kind of walk. Bill had seen me earlier, saying that he and his wife had been separated for several months and he wanted to get back together. He didn't really know what had gone wrong except they had gotten to the place where they spent most of the time hurting each other and that was when Jo Ann decided to leave him.

Well, there *was* one thing he was aware of that had caused trouble between them. On one occasion he had hit her. He knew it was wrong but the anger had gotten so strong inside that he felt he could not control himself. We worked two or three sessions on ways for him to get control of the physical expressions of his anger, and then I asked him to ask his wife to come in with him.

Jo Ann was very hesitant about coming because her parents didn't want her to get back together with Bill. They were afraid he would harm her physically. I asked Jo Ann how Bill would need to change before she would be willing to live with him again. She mentioned, of course, that he would have to learn to control his anger. She told the story of their earlier life together that had been good, and then pinpointed where she thought their relationship had gone sour.

Like most marriages (See "The Three Stages of Marriage") the first stage of their relationship had been enchantment. They were in *love* and they didn't see any faults in each other. Also like most marriages theirs moved from the enchantment stage to the disenchantment stage after a year or so. During this disenchantment stage they began to see each other's faults and were rather shocked. She found he got angry easily, and he discovered she was a rather disorganized housekeeper compared to his mother.

So far, their experience was not unlike most young couples in terms of moving through the enchantment stage. However, their predicament was that they never moved out of the stage of disenchantment into maturity, the stage that provides a more settled atmosphere for conflict resolution and for life together.

Jo Ann said that what started the disenchantment period

# 101 : HURT AND ANGER—KNOWING THE DIFFERENCE

## THE THREE STAGES OF MARRIAGE
and some words and ideas that go with these stages

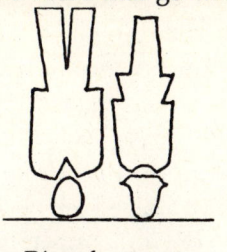

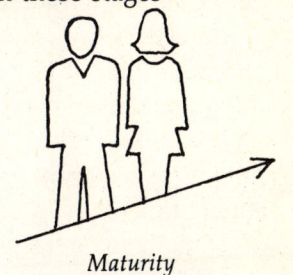

*Enchantment*     *Disenchantment*     *Maturity*

| Enchantment | Disenchantment | Maturity |
|---|---|---|
| On Cloud 9 | Upset | Feet on the ground |
| Perfect | Terrible | I need you |
| Just right | Absolutely wrong | How do you see it? |
| Forever | I quit | Let's work it out |
| Infatuated | Hurt | I'll help you |
| Idolize | Put down | Encourage |
| Numb | Splintered | Whole |
| Fascinated | Irritated | Refreshed |
| Charmed | Wretched | Thankful |
| Captivated | Burdened | Free |
| Ecstasy | Uncomfortable | Comfortable |
| Thrilled | Bitter | Friendly |
| Preoccupied | Trapped | Growing |
| We've arrived | We'll never make it | Together, we can make it |

for her was that Bill began putting her down when they were with friends. They had conflicts they needed to resolve but they didn't talk about these when just the two of them were together. When they had another couple over for an evening, Bill would say things like, "You may have noticed that Jo Ann's not too fond of housework." Jo Ann said this made her very angry, but she didn't know what to do about it, except that usually she just bottled up her feelings and didn't say anything.

As her anger grew, home became a less and less pleasant place, and Bill spent more time with his friends away from home. Jo Ann continued to resent him, but she did not confront him with her feelings. Finally, she moved out.

Anger was the main emotion this young couple displayed and talked about in the early stages of counseling. But as a matter of fact this was not their *primary* predicament. The disenchanting emotion for them, as for most couples, was hurt. When Bill put Jo Ann down in front of others, her almost immediate reaction was a feeling of hurt. As the diagram "The Interaction of Hurt, Anger, and Revengefulness" illustrates, the intensity and awareness of her hurt feelings accelerated rapidly seconds after the personal interaction that caused this. But then anger quickly began to grow more intense. (This is not to say that all anger is caused by hurt. However, this kind of anger seems to cause the most trouble in families, so we are focusing on it.) This feeling of anger eventually peaked out above the emotion of hurt. This dynamic process usually takes place in just a matter of seconds after the incident. A third feeling, the desire to hurt back—revengefulness—often begins to motivate our actions, although we may be only dimly aware of it.

Now it is important to note what happens when persons *back* down into this experience in memory.[1] The first emotion they remember, as they think back to the incident, is not hurt, but the desire for revenge, because that was the last emotion they were aware of. Unless people *have trained themselves* to back on down past the last emotion, they are not aware of the first emotion—hurt. Jo Ann, therefore, was motivated by revenge, and was aware of her anger, but did not seem to be aware of the hurt she had experienced.

I've observed with my counselees and in my own life journey with Lillian that the two most difficult emotions to distinguish are hurt and anger. Because they emerge almost simultaneously and because one overlays the other, we

# HURT AND ANGER—KNOWING THE DIFFERENCE

## THE INTERACTION OF HURT, ANGER AND REVENGEFULNESS

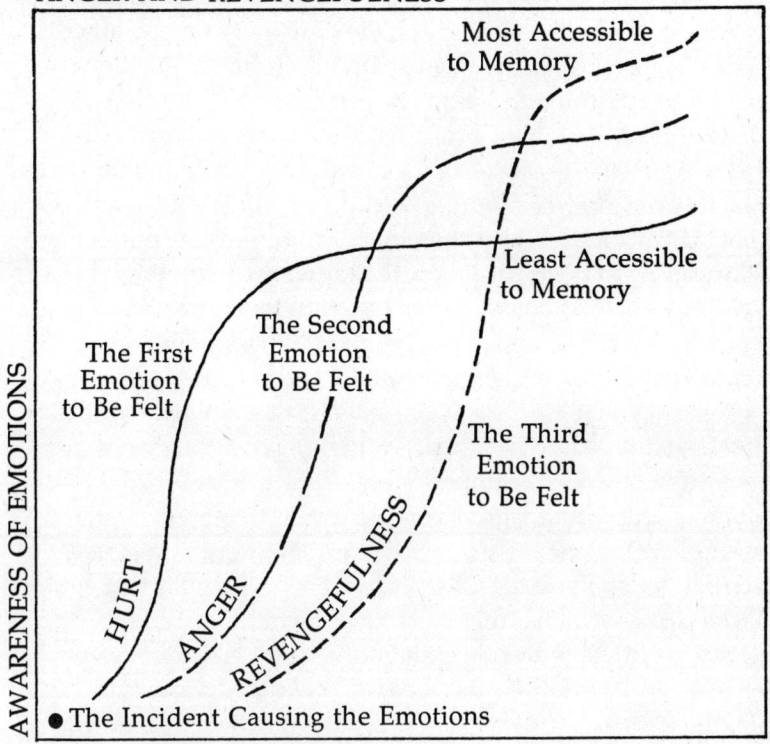

*A graph with "AWARENESS OF EMOTIONS" on the y-axis and "THE PASSING OF TIME" on the x-axis. Three curves rise from "The Incident Causing the Emotions": HURT (The First Emotion to Be Felt, Most Accessible to Memory), ANGER (The Second Emotion to Be Felt), and REVENGEFULNESS (The Third Emotion to Be Felt, Least Accessible to Memory).*

have to be very accurate in taking our emotional pulse to determine which emotion is churning around inside and causing our present behavior.

Most people who have been hurt respond in one of three ways: 1) They tell the other person that what he or she did hurt them, 2) They forgive the other person, or 3) They hurt back. Jo Ann hurt back. She refused to communicate with Bill and she moved out. As we worked together, Bill and Jo Ann moved below the revenge and anger they had directed towards each other, and began to talk about the ways they had hurt each other. As they did this, their sensitivity for the other person grew. After they had shared their hurts, Jo Ann chose to begin living with Bill again.

Bill and Jo Ann are Christians. They were ashamed of what they had done because, as they said, they had not only hurt each other, they had hurt and confused other people around them. They asked what they might do to prevent this from happening in the future because they were still quite shaky about their relationship. I suggested to them that in addition to the Christian disciplines of Bible study, prayer, and church attendance, they maintain a "prime time" each day when they would share as honestly as they knew how, the feelings they had toward each other, positive as well as negative. It would be important to tell each other when they were doing things right as well as when they were doing things wrong. Also I suggested they adopt the rule of *never* criticizing their mate in front of others. Bill would find that it would take considerably more courage to try to resolve conflicts in a one-to-one situation with Jo Ann, than to put her down in front of other people, where she would not fight back.

I suggested that when they did feel the emotion of hurt, they tell their mate as soon as possible and communicate specifically and concretely what had been done to cause the hurt. A good way to keep the hurt from nagging inside is to get it outside. And taking this step makes forgiveness much easier. Also I urged them to get involved in a small group of Christians in their church.

I made a final suggestion to Bill and Jo Ann before they left to begin a new chapter of their adventure together, that is, that they develop a new kind of commitment to each other so they

## 105 : HURT AND ANGER—KNOWING THE DIFFERENCE

did not look on their marriage as they might look on a disposable pop bottle or paper napkin, but rather that they look at their marriage as Jesus did: "So they are no longer two but one. What therefore God has joined together, let no man put asunder" (Matthew 19:6). It would be this commitment, and this view of marriage, that would enable them to move on through the stage of disenchantment and into the stage of maturity.

## Questions

1. Do you remember a time this week when you were angry with another family member?
2. Can you move down in your thinking, below the anger? Do you recall any other feeling prior to the anger? Were you hurt by the incident?
3. Have you shared these feelings with the person involved?

# CHAPTER NINE: A CHRISTIAN—ANGRY?

How does God view the angry Christian? Is anger sinful, or is it a legitimate expression of a God-given emotion? How we answer these questions will make a vital difference in our behavior. For example, parents who never permit their children to express anger have taken the position that anger is wrong and sinful.

Those who are concerned about whether anger is right or wrong are involved in a predicament, because there are evidences for both positions. At first glance, the biblical position regarding anger appears to be equivocal. On the one hand, both the Old Testament (Psalm 4:4) and the New

## 107 : A CHRISTIAN—ANGRY?

Testament (Ephesians 4:26) point out that sin need not necessarily accompany anger, "Be angry, but sin not...." On the other hand, in the same New Testament paragraph (Ephesians 4:31, 32), Christians are told to "let all bitterness and wrath and anger and clamor and slander be put away from you, with all malice, and be kind to one another, tenderhearted, forgiving one another, as God in Christ forgave you." This command indicates that Christians are to separate themselves from anger. How are we to reconcile these two scriptural points of view regarding sin?

If we add our own experience with anger to the scriptural data, we continue to find evidences for conflicting points of view. Take, for example, the effect of our anger upon others. We have all experienced situations in which we have become angry at a friend, or relative, and have thereby weakened our relationship with that person. On the other hand, we have been involved in situations in which we have expressed anger at another person and this expressed anger "cleared the air" and actually helped bring about a stronger relationship between the two of us.

Incidentally, it does not seem to be practical to try to distinguish between anger and the expression of anger, as if one is OK and the other is not. If we are angry, we will express it in one way or another. It eats on our body in some way if we try to bottle it up. Also, the person we are mad at usually is aware of it even if we try to hide it. We express our anger in one way or another, whether we intend to or not.

What about the effect of our anger upon ourselves? In some instances, we feel worse after we have expressed our anger than before. We may feel guilty for treating someone else badly. In other situations, we feel better after getting our anger out. We find that the tightness, discomfort, and generally upset feeling have disappeared.

In summary, therefore, we see that the evidences from Scripture and from our own experience are capable of two different interpretations—anger may be sinful or it may not be. There is a *third* possibility, that whether or not anger is sinful depends upon *how* it is expressed. This third alternative would explain the apparent conflict in scriptural data. If we express our anger in a destructive way, it is wrong from God's point of view. This is the situation in Ephesians 4:31, where this type of angry expression is akin to bitterness, wrath, clamor, slander, and malice. If we can express it in a constructive way, we can be angry "and sin not." This third possibility also explains our experience with our own expressed anger. We typically feel worse after we have expressed our anger in a destructive way, and certainly the person who is the target of our anger feels worse. If we can be constructive in the expression of our anger, the chances are that both we and the other person will feel better when it is all over.

If anger, then, can be either sinful or useful, depending on how we respond to its presence in us, are there some practical suggestions regarding our response to it? The following three guidelines are Bible-based and appear to be borne out by experience. They are expressed as contrasts.

## Slow to Anger Rather Than Easily Offended

Since God the Father is a person, it is helpful to look at his traits and model after them when possible. Some of his traits cannot be copied, of course, such as his omnipresence and omnipotence. Others can be patterned after in our own finite way, such as his love and kindness, and his characteristic of not being easily angered. Psalm 145:8 tells us, "The Lord is gracious and merciful, slow to anger and abounding in

## 109 : A CHRISTIAN—ANGRY?

steadfast love." That we are to follow this pattern is made clear by James 1:19, "Know this, my beloved brethren. Let every man be quick to hear, slow to speak, slow to anger."

There may be some who counter at this point with the fact that we often seem to have no control over how fast we get angry. It is a valid point that we often spontaneously get mad. However, through self-discipline we can become less *easily* angered. For example, a child often has little tolerance for frustration. A "No" from the child's parents may set off a loud display of anger. As the child gets older he learns to accept "No's" from others without becoming angry at all.

The crux of the matter is how easily we are offended. In any interpersonal situation there are four possible outcomes with regard to being offended.

1. *No offense is intended and none is taken.* Fortunately this is the case in most interactions. There is no anger present.

2. *No offense is intended but it is taken.* One is "touchy" or irritable. The only cure for touchiness is love.

3. *An offense is intended and it is taken.* The fight is on! The remedy here, where the offense is intentional, is forgiveness.

4. *An offense is intended but it is not taken.* Some spiritual growth has taken place. Proverbs 19:11 speaks to this situation, "Good sense makes a man slow to anger, and it is his glory to overlook an offense." Forgiveness is not necessary here because the recipient of the offensive remark simply refuses to become offended. This person has worked hard at disciplining himself or herself so that gradually the tolerance level for becoming offended is raised. A sense of humor helps here. If we take ourselves too seriously, we become offended very easily. A firm sense of our own worth as a child of God helps, too, because if we have this, we are less likely to feel injured by the abrasiveness of others.

If we are willing to work at it, perhaps it is possible to gain control over anger in the same way we gain control over the tendency to judge others. Jesus said in Matthew 7:1 that we are not to judge others. Yet we often seem to spontaneously judge another person in the same way we feel anger spontaneously emerging. However, we may have more control over both than we think. The key to reducing our judging of others seems to be the amount of work we are willing to invest in understanding them. If we invest a great deal of time and energy in understanding other persons, we are much less likely to make snap judgments about them. By striving, as St. Francis of Assisi has prayed, "not so much to be understood, as to understand," we will arrive at the place where we are not easily angered.

But suppose we have become angry. Let's say that sin was not involved because we were not easily angered. There was a considerable stimulus that caused our angry response. What do we do now?

## Short-term Anger Rather Than Long-term Hostility

Again, we find God the Father as the model for anger being only a *temporary* state: "For his anger is but for a moment, and his favor is for a lifetime" (Psalm 30:5a). The Christian is instructed in Ephesians 4:26 to follow this example, "Be angry but do not sin; do not let the sun go down on your anger." The implication here is that it is sinful to permit ourselves to *stay* angry. The reason that this is so is that anger which is continued turns into hostility. A. T. Jersild has defined hostility as "a lingering or residual form of potential anger that persists beyond the occasion."[1] He further notes some symptoms of hostility:

## 111 : A CHRISTIAN—ANGRY?

> Attitudes of hostility ... may prevail in the form
> of grievances or a chronic disposition to have a chip
> on one's shoulder. They may appear in a tendency to
> be sarcastic. They may prevail in the form of prejudices,
> or in a tendency to bristle or rebel (or to cringe) when
> dealing with an authority figure, or in a tendency to
> become angered by little annoyances that,
> objectively, do not merit so much wrath.[2]

Hostility, if not dealt with, can become a way of life. There are some people whose lives can be characterized by the one word, "hostile," just as there are some people whose life can be summed up by the word "miserly." Hostility is to be avoided because it always causes suffering for the hostile person and those close to him.

We can shorten the life span of our anger by refusing to nourish it. The phrase "nourishing a grudge" is a familiar one. We nourish a grudge when we attribute bad intentions to the person with whom we are angry. Or we may spend a great deal of "head time" on the incident that caused our anger. By going over and over it in our minds, we gradually warp our memory of it and become madder and madder at the other person involved in the incident that is now distorted in our memory.

Hostility is damaging to others and may actually shorten our own lives. A recent book by two cardiologists, *Type A Behavior and Your Heart*, identifies hostility as one of the "Type A" behaviors that are symptomatic of stress, and contribute to elevated cholesterol and heart disease. This hostility often shows up as impatience and irritability as the following clues indicate:

> If you feel (particularly if you openly exhibit to
> others) an impatience with the rate at which most
> events take place. You are suffering from this sort of
> impatience if you find it difficult to restrain yourself

from hurrying the speech of others...
Other signs of this sort of impatience: if you become *unduly* irritated or even enraged when a car ahead of you in your lane runs at a pace you consider too slow; if you find it anguishing to wait in a line or to wait your turn to be seated at a restaurant...[3]

This added evidence from the field of medicine tends to confirm the point of view that hostility can become a way of life. If we discover hostility within ourselves, we need to look for ways to get rid of our anger more quickly. One such way to make our anger short-lived is to express it in a constructive way. This is further explained in the third guideline.

## Communication Rather Than Revenge

The Bible is quite clear concerning revenge:

Repay no one evil for evil, but take thought for what is noble in the sight of all. If possible, so far as it depends upon you, live peaceably with all. Beloved, never avenge yourselves, but leave it to the wrath of God; for it is written, "Vengeance is mine, I will repay, says the Lord."[4]

Revenge is simply hurting someone back who has hurt us, or who we believe hurt us. As noted in the diagram on page 103, there is a close and easily confused relationship among hurt, anger, and revengefulness. It is quite possible to hurt someone back and never be aware of it.

Should anger be shared? Yes, if we mean by this that we tell the person with whom we are angry how we are feeling and what caused it, if we know. When we communicate the fact that we are angry, we often experience a draining away of the anger. If we bottle it up, it keeps nagging us.

Communicating our anger frees us from *acting it out*.

When we act out our anger we usually cause another person to suffer in some way. One middle-aged man and woman who had been married for many years experienced this predicament over lawn work. Because he was slow to get at the spring work on the lawn, she reminded him of the work that needed to be done. He took offense at the reminders which he considered nagging, became grouchy with her, and said things to her which hurt. He acted out rather than stated his anger. When he found the courage to tell her he was angry with her, he got over his anger! He also started to work on the lawn.

Courage is the key characteristic in communicating our anger. We usually get angry with people we care about and are close to, rather than with strangers. Now it takes a considerable amount of courage to tell a loved one that we are angry with him or her. It doesn't take any courage to act out our anger by hurting that person. Where do we find the courage to face our loved one and share our anger? Perhaps from the conviction that our hidden anger is weakening our love relationship and we will not allow that to continue.

## Love As a Deterrent to Anger

Most anger comes from being frustrated or becoming offended. Frustration usually involves an impersonal anger, and taking offense involves a personal anger—becoming angry at a person. If one is expecting to be promoted in a job and fails to receive a promotion because there is a financial cutback in the company and an administrative position is eliminated, one may be frustrated and, as a result, very angry. On the other hand, if a promotion I want is given to my rival, I may find myself getting angry at him, or at my superior who made the decision.

One New Testament passage speaks to both becoming

frustrated and becoming offended, "Love does not insist on its own way; it is not irritable or resentful."[5] It is when we have to have things our own way that we become frustrated. When we begin to lessen this insistence on having things our way, we find a greater release from anger caused by frustration. And it is when we are irritable or resentful that we are especially subject to becoming offended by another person. As we gradually incorporate love into our life style, the sources of our anger are diminished. They are not eliminated, however, so we face the challenge of dealing with our anger (and others' anger) now and then. If we follow the above guidelines in those situations, we may find the sharing of anger, although painful, can serve to bring us closer together.

## Questions

1. In comparison with others whom you know, do you become easily offended, or does it take a lot to make you angry?
2. Do you typically remain angry longer than a day?
3. Do you usually communicate your anger, or act it out?

# CHAPTER TEN: IF HE'D JUST—ONCE—LISTEN TO ME!

Onna clenched her fists and moved her forearms up and down rapidly as she said, "If he'd just —*once*—listen to me!" I mentioned to her that her arm and hand action looked as if she would like to shake him. She said she *would* like to—"Maybe I could get his attention that way."

## Powerlessness, Anger, and Violence

Donna's anger and her imaginary shaking of her husband came from her sense of *powerlessness*. She couldn't get him to listen to her. She had tried and tried but she felt she could not get him to attend to what she wanted him to hear. Now she was angry and the thought had crossed her mind, at least subconsciously, of using violence—only a small amount, to be sure.

Rollo May, a New York City psychoanalyst, has spent many years studying the relationship of powerlessness and violence. He has concluded that powerlessness corrupts people.

> For violence has its breeding ground in impotence and apathy. True, aggression has been so often and so regularly escalated into violence that anyone's discouragement and fear of it can be understood. But what is *not* seen is that the state of powerlessness, which leads to apathy and which can be produced by the above plans for the uprooting of aggression, is the source of violence. As we make people powerless, we promote their violence rather than its control.[1]

This is a directly opposite point of view than many of us as Christians have taken. We are likely to quote the saying, "All power tends to corrupt and absolute power corrupts absolutely." But May quotes Edgar Friedenberg, "All weakness tends to corrupt, and impotence corrupts absolutely."[2]

Now, as another psychoanalyst, Karl Menninger, has pointed out in his book, *Whatever Happened to Sin?*[3] sin emerges in unlikely places and unlikely ways. *Could it be* that we are tempted to sin as much by powerlessness as by power? One of Rollo May's favorite illustrations of the way powerlessness can lead to violence is the main character in Herman Melville's short novel, *Billy Budd*. [4]

Billy Budd is a young, handsome, innocent sailor. He has two predicaments. One, his stuttering, has always been with him. The other, a petty officer who has decided to make

## 117 : IF HE'D JUST—ONCE—LISTEN TO ME!

Billy Budd's life miserable, is the cause of a new predicament, and one that puzzles as well as angers him. Finally, the petty officer, after harassing Billy mercilessly, accuses Billy before the Captain on a trumped-up charge. The Captain instructs Billy to reply to the charge and give his version. Billy, because his speech blockage becomes more severe when he is highly emotional, cannot respond. The petty oficer then makes further untrue accusations. Billy, unable to talk, hits him with all the rage that has been building up from his predicaments. The blow had so much force behind it that it kills the petty officer. Billy then stands trial for murder. Before the sentence of hanging is reluctantly determined by the Captain, Billy Budd says he knows it was wrong to do what he did, but that he wouldn't have hit him had he been able to talk. He became violent, in other words, because he was powerless to say what he needed and wanted to say.

This story, the significance of which was so insightfully pointed out by Rollo May, brings us back to Donna. As she worked her hands and arms in a way that showed she wanted to shake her husband, she was saying the same thing as Billy Budd, that is, "I feel powerless to say what I need to say to him!" The impatience, irritation, resentment, anger, rage, and possibility of violence follow. When *words* fail, what is the next step? Do you have a memory of someone holding you down, perhaps as a child, by pinning your wrists to the floor or ground? Can you remember the feeling of helplessness—and rage?

## Feelings about Power

Do we *want* the power to talk to the members of our family in such a way that they *will* listen? Is it possible we

## 118 : HURT AND ANGER

both want and don't want power? We want it because it would help us get out of our predicament of feeling helpless. On the other hand, if we are helpless we don't have any responsibilities, and there's something inviting about that. Assuming the responsibility for power is an awesome feeling. Then, too, there may be the nagging thought, is it really all right for a Christian to have power? How does power fit in with humility and meekness?

## What Does the Bible Say about Power?

There is at least one reference in Scripture, Zechariah 4:6, that seems at first glance to put power down, "This is the word of the Lord to Zerubbabel: Not by might, nor by power, but by my Spirit, says the Lord of hosts." However, the backdrop for this discussion is national power, and battles between armies. We use a similar expression today, "The great powers of the world," meaning the strongest nations. God is saying in this passage, not that power is unimportant, but rather that the only real power is from the Spirit of God, not from armies.

As a matter of fact, the Bible says it is "lovers of self, lovers of money, proud, arrogant ... lovers of pleasure rather than lovers of God," who are "holding the form of religion but denying the power of it."[5]

There are many other indications from Scripture that God wants us not to deny power, but to take hold of it. The Apostle Paul, in his sign-off to the Romans, writes, "Now to him who is able to strengthen you according to my gospel and the preaching of Jesus Christ..."[6] Jesus said, "Ask, and it will be given you; seek, and you will find; knock, and it will be opened to you."[7] This sounds like power. Paul prayed for the

Colossians, "May you be strengthened with all power, according to his glorious might, for all endurance and patience with joy."[8] He describes this power in another letter, "That I may know him and the power of his resurrection, and may share his sufferings, becoming like him in his death, that if possible I may attain the resurrection from the dead."[9] The power that we have access to, then, is the power of the resurrection itself. This is enough power to say what we need to, to those around us without resorting to anger, rage, and violence. But if we have felt weak, and now we want to claim this power, we may find ourselves, as well as others, changing.

## Some Characteristics of the Powerful Person

As I think of the persons I know who are powerful because they have claimed the resurrection power of Jesus Christ, several common traits are apparent. One aspect of their communication style is that they seem to talk when they need to. This usually has required some changing. For the person who used words to cover his weakness, and who talked about everything to avoid talking about what he needed to, the change has been that he now talks less—and says more. For the person who used silence to cover weakness and who was always quiet ("I'm a good listener"), the change has been that he now talks more.

The powerful person is typically a gentle person. And gentleness shows up in the *choice* of words. A person who is feeling powerless may resort to verbal violence in either the content of what he says (obscenities or profanity) or the way in which he says it (yelling, for example). The truly powerful person does not need to resort to either of these methods to get people to listen to him.

A third characteristic of the powerful person is that the people he is with come away strengthened. Some of his power flows across to the other person. This makes sense because it is the same power the Lord had. And whenever people went to him, they came away stronger, healed, or made whole. The powerful person leaves people stronger than he found them.

## Hurt, Anger, and Power

So far we have seen that in order to avoid getting hung up on anger, we need to 1) be able to distinguish it from hurt, and 2) claim power. How does this work in a concrete situation?

A young couple decided to go on a week's vacation together, and leave their two preschool children with the grandparents. Both the husband and wife were tired and pressured when they left because of the extra work they had to do to get ready. Things went badly. She complained about the motel he chose. He complained about the kind of entertainment she chose. Because they couldn't please each other and because by this time they weren't talking much, they tried to guess what the other person wanted, so they often did what neither of them wanted. Whereas they left tired and pressured, they came home tired and angry. That night after they got the children to bed, the explosion came. As they were yelling at each other, he pushed her backward, hard, and she slapped him, hard. They were both so shocked that they had pushed and hit each other that they called me and said they had to talk that night. They had never angrily laid hands on each other before.

As they told their story, they began to put together what they had done. They left on vacation tired and therefore were more susceptible to stress. When they complained about the other's choices, this criticism hurt the other person. Neither one really intended to hurt the other's feelings. But neither person had the power to confront the other saying, "When you [said or did a certain thing] I really felt hurt." So the anger came and overlaid the hurt, and it was the anger that kept pushing into their awareness until finally they chose to hurt back—first verbally, then physically. At the end of the counseling session they made a commitment to find the courage to tell the other person at the moment they felt hurt what it was in the interchange that hurt them. In this way they would be able to head off their anger.

## Building Sensitivity in the Other Person

One of the forces that moves people into the disenchantment phase of marriage is the discovery that the other person is insensitive to their needs or desires. It's then that the feeling comes—"If he'd just listen to me!" Or it may be that other members of the family are involved. A parent may feel a child is insensitive to his needs, or a child may have the same feelings about one or both of the parents.

How do you make another person more sensitive to you? Many people rely on their expression of anger to do this. But even though anger is the most used feedback system it is not a very efficient one. It is too general and global in nature. Also the other person usually becomes angry at us, and angry people typically aren't open to becoming more sensitive. This is not to say we should never express anger. Sometimes we need to; it is usually healthier than bottling it up. But we should not fool ourselves that it will teach the other person something. I remember one time one of my children slapped a mosquito on her arm and said, "There, that'll teach you a lesson!" But a dead mosquito can't learn. It may be that we are sometimes more destructive than educational when we try to teach a family member "a lesson" when we are angry.

There are at least two effective ways I know of to make other persons more sensitive to my needs. First, I can tell them when they have done something that hurts me. This requires strength for me to do this. I have never found it easy. And to be helpful in the feedback process, I have to specify exactly what the other person has done to cause the hurt. I still remember an incident that occurred over thirty years ago, when I was in the eighth grade in a little country school in Kansas. A good friend, who was smaller than I, was scuffling with me during recess. I remember I was pulling on his arm when an expression of pain came on his face, and he said, "Paul, that hurt!" That feedback taught me what it was to hurt somebody I liked very much. It was a strong, effective lesson that has lasted all these years.

A second way I can make people more sensitive to my needs is to tell them when they do something I really like. People need to know when they do something right as well as when they do something wrong. In fact, we can far more effectively change another person's behavior by informing them when they do something right, than telling them when they do something wrong. One summer I filled in for various people in a department store as they went on vacation. Because each person's task was new to me from week to week, I almost always lacked the skills I needed. But I knew I'd really had it the week the display man left for vacation. For some reason I couldn't make a display look like the plans showed it should. But I gritted my teeth and built my first window

## 123 : IF HE'D JUST—ONCE—LISTEN TO ME!

display. It was supposed to advertise hardware items which were to go on sale that week. I finished it and went around in front of the store to look at it. There was another person there also looking at the window. He told me he was the display manager for all the stores in the entire region. I said something like, "Oh." He looked it over pretty thoroughly, and then he turned to me and said, "It's stupid." That set off all kinds of emotions in me. I felt like hitting him; I felt like saying, "I knew it first." Mostly I felt like getting out of there—but I was married and had two little children and I needed the job. So, like Billy Budd, I didn't say anything.

His remark did lots of things to me, but one thing it didn't do, it didn't teach me how to display hardware items effectively. After he left, the hardware manager came over to the window and said something like, "I like the way you have that power saw placed; I wonder how these other items would look if we changed them this way?" So he helped me build the display by getting involved in the activity with me. I appreciated his patience and kindness, and the gentle way he taught me by starting with the one thing I had done right.

I think the lesson I learned from this painful experience was how to correct a person without hurting him. When we are working with our children, we need to start with what they are doing right and go from there. Parents who have used the display manager's technique have discovered, often too late, that it has damaged their relationship with their child. It is important that parents encourage children. The transaction is that as the adult gives encouragement, the child takes courage. Again, this calls for the parents to be powerful. Children draw their strength from the powerful adults around them.

"May you be strengthened with all power, according to his glorious might, for all endurance and patience with joy."[10]

## Questions

1. Do your family members listen to you?
2. Are you powerful enough to get their attention?
3. If not, are you willing to claim the power that Christ has promised?
4. Is there someone in your family you feel is not very sensitive to your needs? If so, what is your plan for building that person's sensitivity?

# CHAPTER ELEVEN: GETTING PAST THE BRISTLES

In the last chapter we looked at some ways of getting *ourselves* out of the predicament of hurt and anger. Now we'll look at some ways of *helping another person* out of this kind of predicament. If there is a person in your family who is hurting, or angry—or both—you will have a reasonably good chance of helping them if you follow these three steps: 1) *Work on yourself,* so that you are not defensive; 2) *Work on building the relationship* with the other person, so that you are close enough to help; and 3) *Work on the predicament together,* so you are viewed as a helper, not as someone who is interfering.

## How to Work on Yourself

This step and the second step are the most often overlooked approaches in trying to help an angry person. And they are by far the most important steps. The person in this predicament almost always bristles with unexpressed (and sometimes outward) anger, and we can't get past the bristles if we don't do our homework on the first two steps.

We have to work on ourselves first so that we do not react defensively to the other person's anger. If we become defensive we usually bristle, and two prickly people can't get close enough to give and receive help. Many books have described the defense mechanisms, such as projection, rationalization, and repression, in an effort to study defensiveness. I've found them interesting to study but of very little use in changing my behavior or the behavior of others. We'll try a different, and hopefully a more practical approach.

We'll use a monitoring technique to discover and reduce our defensiveness. By monitoring, I mean a careful observation of oneself and others. It differs from analyzing. When we analyze something we have done, we are usually trying to figure out *why* we did it. Psychoanalysis is based on the medical model of finding out why a condition exists.

In monitoring, we are not trying to figure out *why* we are defensive. We are concerned with the answer to the question, "What?" In fact, we will be concerned with the answer to three "What" questions: 1) What is my body doing? 2) What action am I taking toward the other person? and 3) What is the other person doing in reaction to me?

## Monitoring My Body

How aware are we of what our body is telling us concerning our defensiveness? Do we always know when

# 127 : GETTING PAST THE BRISTLES

## WHAT'S HAPPENING IN MY BODY?

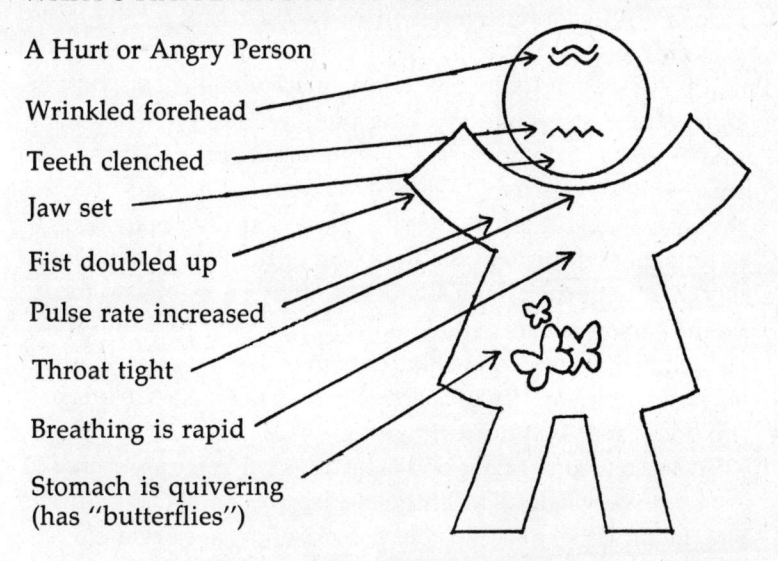

A Hurt or Angry Person

Wrinkled forehead

Teeth clenched

Jaw set

Fist doubled up

Pulse rate increased

Throat tight

Breathing is rapid

Stomach is quivering (has "butterflies")

we are angry? One time when I was teaching in high school, a teacher walking along the hall caught my attention. He was pulling a student by the neck to the office. The student's face looked as if he were in some pain so I told the teacher, a friend of mine, to let the student go—I was sure he would go to the office on his own. (That particular student had been sent to the office so many times that he felt rather at home there.) Later I asked the teacher why he had gotten so angry. He looked quite surprised and said, "Angry? I wasn't angry." I replied that his face was flushed at the time, the veins on his neck were standing out, his arm muscles were bulging, and his hands were gripping the boy's neck so tightly, I was wondering if the boy was able to breathe adequately. At this, the teacher got mad at me, but he was sincerely unaware of his anger at the boy. I've wondered since how many times *I've* been unaware of defensive, angry feelings I've had, because I wasn't in touch with my own body.

Notice in the drawing, "What's Happening in My Body?" that there are many changes taking place when we are hurt or angry. If I can feel energy being pumped into my body in such a way as to prepare me to fight (argue) or run, then I am reacting defensively. There may be a quivering in the stomach or a tightness in the chest, or a clenching of the teeth, or an almost imperceptible doubling of the fist. How do we work with our own defensiveness so that we are free to focus on the person who is in the predicament of hurt and anger? A guideline is that *we work with that part of ourselves where we have pinpointed the defensiveness.* Since in this instance it is in the body, we need to work with the body.

To get in control of our body reactions when we are scared or mad, one very helpful technique is deep breathing. We simply stop talking, listen to the other person, and take several *slow, deep* breaths. This exercise almost always has a quieting, restful effect on our body. We are then free again to focus on the needs of the other person.

## Monitoring My Actions toward the Other Person

We need to be very aware of the interaction between ourselves and the other person. The first aspect of this interaction has to do with what we are saying and doing. For example, are we saying something to explain ourselves or justify our position? If we are, it is likely we are feeling defensive. If our son or daughter asks us for the car keys and we deny this request, then follow it up by saying something like, "Well, when I was a boy I walked nearly everywhere—I even walked two miles to school and back home," the chances are we are feeling defensive. Fortunately, our children usually bring us back to reality. One time I referred to how far I used to walk to school during my growing-up days back in Kansas. One of my children to whom I was explaining my youthful hardships said, "Dad, as nearly as I can tell, *everyone* your age walked two miles to school. The way I figure it, they built the schoolhouse first and then built all the houses on a two-mile radius in a circle around it." That was the last time I used that particular reference with my children to try to justify some position or other.

If we catch ourselves saying something with an "edge" on it to the other person, the chances are we are feeling hurt and we are trying to hurt back, or we are feeling powerless to get the person to do what we want him to do. For example, if we say, "Well, I've noticed your sister always sits right down after dinner and does her homework," our hope is to motivate or manipulate the resistant child to begin to study. However, this remark usually *increases* the resistance to the homework because the statement came across as a put-down.

What should we do if we discover ourselves explaining our explanations, justifying a position with weak evidences, or putting another family member down? Remember, the basic rule is that we work with that part of ourselves where the problem is. If it is in our body, we work with our body. If it is in our communication, we straighten out our communication. We *admit* that the distance we walked to school really doesn't have a close connection to a request for car keys. We apologize if we hurt a child in an effort to arouse the competitive spirit. Then we get at the real issue, whatever that is. Maybe, in the latter case, we can work out together a suitable time for study or maybe we as parents will simply need to require a certain time for study. At least this is a straightforward approach.

## What Is the Other Person Doing in Reaction to Me?

We need to monitor not only our body and our actions, but also the reactions of the other person. By observing the other person closely we can gauge our own defensiveness. If the other person "distances" himself physically by backing off or looking out the window, or removes himself psychologically by "tuning us out," he may be telling us we are making him uncomfortable. There are times that may be necessary, if we are confronting him; on the other hand, it may be that we have become angry without knowing it, and he is feeling attacked. Another clue to our anger is the other person's sudden aggressiveness toward us for (apparently) no reason. If the other person suddenly becomes angry with us, we need to take our emotional pulse and see how we are feeling. Were we hurt or angry first?

When we become upset or angry, the other person often feels attacked. Most people react to an attack by either flight or fight. If they "distance" themselves from us, they may be taking *flight*, even if they move back only a foot or two. If they become aggressive (for example, yell at us), they are choosing the *fight* option. By looking for these two basic reactions, we may get an important clue to our own defensive actions.

So, what do we do if we are getting clues that the other person is feeling attacked by us, that is, that we are reacting defensively? Now before making a suggestion here, I want to emphasize that most of the time when we are coming across defensive to the other person, we won't *feel* defensive. We *cannot* trust our feelings at this point. We are not aware of our defense mechanisms until we get feedback. That is why the three guidelines for determining our defensiveness center on *behaviors, not feelings*. We must observe our body, our actions

# 131 : GETTING PAST THE BRISTLES

and communication, and the other person's reactions.

Now back to the "So what" question—so we observe the other person's reactions, then what do we do? If the other person has either a flight or fight reaction, we need to respond, as before, in the area of the clue. A response might be, "I noticed that you backed off when I said that. Did you feel I was jumping on you?" or "Your voice is now much louder. Do you feel I'm really not listening to you?" In other words, we need to say what the other person's action was that caused our conclusion about him.

Well, let's assume that we have learned to become aware of our own defensiveness and to reduce it. We need a great deal of determination and patience here because just when we think we have our defensiveness licked, it bounces back and gives us a tough fight. But, let's say we are making progress in working with ourselves. Now we need to work on building a stronger relationship with the other person.

## How to Build a Relationship

Following are several guidelines that may be helpful in building relationship:

1. *Do not hurry another member of your family unnecessarily.* I was traveling this last weekend. As I entered a men's room in a restaurant along Interstate 80, I noticed a man sending his boy (probably about six or seven years old) into one of the stalls. His instruction was: "Now hurry up!" I remember thinking, "There are some things we should not have to hurry at!"

Today a mother talked to me about her seven-year-old: "One of her problems is she eats so slowly; she likes to talk when she eats." I suggested the problem would be more severe if her daughter gobbled her food without saying a word. Table fellowship occupies an important place in the New Testament. The Lord took time to talk as he ate.

Hurrying another family member tends to weaken a relationship. We may gain a few extra minutes a day, but perhaps the price is too high. Is it possible that we have overprogrammed ourselves? As we slow our pace, we will find more time for people.

2. *Treat the members of your family with courtesy.* Someone has said that most people treat their guests better than their family. We often work harder at building a relationship with persons outside the family than in the family. Perhaps we take members of our family for granted and don't work on these relationships. A very simple rule, and one that would result in greatly improved relationships, is "Be friendly to family." The reason for a rule like this is that most people overlook the obvious. I stopped by to visit with a young man this evening. He was very friendly and hospitable to me. He and his wife have a six-year-old boy and are expecting another child. While I was there, his boy got into his tool box and the young father said to him, "I hope your brother or sister isn't like you. I couldn't take another one like you." The boy reacted with a hurt, then an angry, expression. The father had been unfriendly with his boy instead of simply correcting him regarding the tool box.

3. *Get the dialogue going.* One time before going to bed, I went into one of my children's bedrooms and sat on the edge of the bed. He asked me to rub his back, and we talked as we got in touch in this way. I asked him to tell me about his day, which he did. Then I was pleasantly surprised when he said, "Now tell me about your day, Dad." Getting in touch helped us begin the dialogue, then the dialogue helped us grow closer. Some suggestions for dialogue "starters" and "continuers" were given in Chapter 3. It may be helpful to review these

suggestions at this point.

4. *Rebuild the relationship when necessary.* It is possible that a relationship can be weakened so much that it must be rebuilt. I have never seen any relationship rebuilt without the element of sacrifice present on the part of at least one of the involved persons. The model for this transaction is, of course, Jesus Christ, who by his sacrifice made possible the rebuilding of the relationship between man and God. To restore a broken family relationship we may have to be willing to sacrifice time, a job, money, pride, some "ideal" we have in our head or something else very close to us.

## How to Work on the Predicament Together

If we have worked hard on the first two steps of changing ourselves and strengthening the relationship with the other person, this third step will be much easier. In this stage of working on the predicament, we need to try to strengthen the other person. All we have to work with is his strength. If he feels very weak, it is like trying to push a wet noodle to get him going on the predicament. He will draw his strength from you, but it will take something out of you when this happens.

We need to keep reminding ourselves that we cannot resolve a predicament *for* another person. We can only work on it *with* him. This means that we must leave the responsibility with the other family member. Jesus gave a straight response to the rich young ruler concerning what he needed to do to inherit the kingdom of God. However, he allowed the young man to make his own choice regarding the matter. On another occasion, when Martha asked Jesus to intervene with Mary, Jesus faced Martha with her responsibility. We do not do the other family member a favor when we take away his or her responsibility for the predicament.

It is also important to keep remembering that advice doesn't work in a predicament. When we are working closely with the other person we will be able to see that he has already considered nearly all the avenues suggested long before the advice was given. Predicaments are too complex to yield to easy solutions.

Finally, it is very important to realize that when a family member is hurting, he will not be very aware of others. Such a person is too busy feeling his own hurt to tune in to where other people are coming from. We may have to interpret this to other family members.

## Questions

1. How effectively do you monitor your own defensiveness?
2. Do you typically hurry other family members at tasks? If so, is it helping?
3. With whom in your family do you have the strongest relationship? The weakest?

# four: depression

*The depressed person is caught
in the cobweb of painful
past memories.*

*How can we go about pulling
him loose and bringing him
into the present?*

# CHAPTER TWELVE: THE DARK NIGHT OF THE SOUL

The letter from Ann, a counselee, read as follows:

> Sometimes I think it would help for you to really know my feelings and what goes on in my head and heart in between visits. Maybe this would help our visits more... It seems to me life has become a hardship, something to be endured—knowing I'll never be truly happy again, but being willing to accept just enough to get by and keep going. Things that once were a joy and an excitement to me are just there, not to be enjoyed, but just there....
>
> Sometimes I get real scared, wondering about God. He used to be my Comforter but now he *seems* to be

my judge. I know he never changes, but I did. Everyone tells me I'm leaving God out, that he can and will mend and repair and heal the hurt, only if "I" allow him to do so. Where have I fallen away?...

I am too afraid to take my life, but equally afraid to live life.[1]

Ann was a gifted, intelligent Christian, with a husband who cared for her, and with growing children. Her pastor referred her to me because she was depressed. She had been to see me twice. A few days after the second session she sent me the above letter, describing her battle with depression.

## What Is Depression Like?

In terms of feelings the depressed person is *sad*, in terms of behavior he is *inactive*, and in terms of communication, he tends to *depreciate* himself. Ann's letter illustrates these three characteristics. The sadness comes through when she says, "... life has become a hardship, something to be endured." Often the sadness has a hopelessness that goes along with it, as shown by the words, "knowing I'll never be truly happy again...." The word "never" functions as a window through which one can see the terrible feeling of hopelessness which many depressed persons have.

This hopeless feeling leads to the second characteristic of inactivity. If things are *never* going to get any better, why work at life? Ann's initiative was gone. She felt life was to be endured. Now endurance is a Christian virtue, but it should not make up our total approach to life. Many active verbs are used in Scripture regarding our life style, such as "fight," "work," "love," and "give." But the depressed person lacks energy and drive.

This inactivity promotes the third characteristic of depression—self-depreciation. When Ann failed to care for her children and her husband, she felt guilty, and began to put herself down. This led to further inaction, and the downward spiral accelerated until she reached her low point.

## The Deep River

Later, when Ann was well on her way on the journey back to health, she agreed to share her letters as well as to tell in more detail some of that journey. She described the "low point" mentioned above.

> I can remember at first I used to feel like I was in a deep, dark pit, unable to pull myself up. Everything seemed hazy and more than I could take. I hated for mornings to come because it meant I had to face another day and I felt I couldn't face even that. I would wake up saying over and over things that degraded myself, like how stupid I was, a lot of "why" questions that couldn't be answered and the fact I knew I couldn't face another day. Evenings proved to be easier because I knew I could go to sleep and forget.
>
> When you don't love yourself, it's impossible to love anyone else. Evidently there was this way of feeling about myself before, not loving myself and it became evident during the depression.
>
> My husband suffered, I'm sure, more than I know. For one thing, he began to feel like every decision he made was wrong... And now he was having to make decisions for me as I wasn't capable. My children suffered, too. They knew Mom was sick and always wondered when I would fall apart again....
>
> During all this time I was unable to discipline the children and it soon became very evident they were frustrated at my weakness, too. They cried a lot, fought with each other and were very restless.[2]

At about this time, it became necessary to hospitalize Ann for about a month. She needed a "time-out" from her responsibilities and she needed intensive counseling. Later she pointed out that before she entered the hospital

> I was very suicidal. The only way out I could see was to end it all. I would devise ways in my mind to do it. No matter how long and furious people talked about what it would do to my kids, the thought was too much a part of my thinking process. It seemed like everything had ended for me, there was no sense in anything, my home and family meant nothing. There was no use in anything anymore...
>
> The month I spent at (the hospital), I feel was only profitable because I had no choice but to get away from my environment. I was expecting a real Christian emphasis, which wasn't there, much to my dismay. But I did learn many valuable lessons there. My problem, although I was saved, was still a very human problem. One doctor there told me it was as if I was going through a deep river and the only way out was to go through and it would probably be deeper in the middle. I wanted someone to snatch me so I wouldn't have to work my way through. I learned from other people, Christian or not, because they were human and so was I....[3]

The first part of Ann's stay at the hospital was very trying for her. Her letter to me at the end of the first week closed with the following two sentences:

> The young kids and a lot of others talk so filthy and sometimes I just can't believe I'm in such a place.
> Do you really feel I can profit from such a place?[4]

I replied by return mail that I was sure she could profit from this experience, and I suggested she work at loving the young kids. Later she wrote me again from the hospital:

## 141 : THE DARK NIGHT OF THE SOUL

> As you could tell, I was very discouraged at the time I wrote you. It's amazing that all the things you bring out in your letter are things the Lord is gradually showing me. The Lord is showing me I've had a very narrow view of what other Christians should be. Yes, God is using other human beings to make a difference in my life. It comes to me over and over what you told me about being a Christian, but not resigning from the human race....
>
> And guess what?—those "filthy talking kids," I've really learned to *love*. I've learned from these kids some reasons why they're in the situation they are in, and a lot stems back to their parents, and the Lord has really "pounded home" to me how I need to be really spending time with my children teaching them, loving them, letting them know they are special. I guess I never thought I was too special myself, so it was hard to make them think they're something special....
>
> It's real strange how I've always pretty much prided myself on accepting people the way they are, but I really had a rude awakening as to how prejudiced I really am.
>
> I have had some sessions with some very good counselors. The Lord is teaching me a lot and the change is coming, I know it and I can feel it and I'm really excited about going home and starting to live again.
>
> Thank you again for your letter and your prayers.[5]

So, Ann made it through the middle of the deep river. She did it not only by receiving help from others, but also by giving help to the youth at the hospital. It took a great deal of courage, effort, and love for her to reach out to others when she was hurting herself, but she chose to do it. And she found in reaching out to help that she began to find health for herself.

Even though Ann had moved through the deepest part of the river, she was not across it yet. After she returned home

## 142 : DEPRESSION

from the hospital, she continued her weekly counseling sessions. There were times when she still focused on the past. In one of her letters during this time, she wrote:

> Please, Dr. Welter, pray with me that I get sickened of tearing apart the past and start looking forward to the future. All the past does is tear me down and I want to go on living.[6]

Somehow she found the strength not to give up. Some of that strength came from other Christians. As she looked back on this time later, she recalled that

> if it hadn't been for other Christians encouraging me, I don't know where I'd be. One Christian man who went through a very deep depression years ago told me when I came to the end of the rope and couldn't take it any longer, to tie a knot and hang on. And many, many times that's all I could do was hang on with the hope that someday things would be better.
>
> I really believed I didn't deserve to be happy again or to enjoy anyone or anything anymore because I had made too many mistakes. Through counseling I began to see the things I said I couldn't do were actually things I wouldn't do, so I had to literally force myself to do things I feared and wouldn't do. I was told doing comes before feeling. I found myself enjoying different things, but always the thought would come, "You can't enjoy that, you don't deserve to." As I forced myself to do the things I feared most, mainly living, I soon found I could enjoy different things and people in spite of myself. As time went on, and time is the best healer, my panicky feeling gradually went away and I found gradually I wasn't dwelling on the past and my failures as much.[7]

I noticed on the next to the last visit with Ann that she had made a dramatic improvement in the way she was functioning. She was going to church again, she called the

## 143 : THE DARK NIGHT OF THE SOUL

Vacation Bible School director to offer her services, and she went with her family and another family to a concert. She said she had decided, "I'm going to live so I may as well work at it."

In the early part of this chapter, I defined depression as including sadness, inactivity, and self-depreciation. Ann was now finding ways to win over all three of these characteristics, as her explanation below shows:

> The day I woke up and didn't get mad because the sun was shining and the day I decided I wanted to start fixing myself up again helped me to see that I was starting to mend again. Another thing I was doing which is definitely destructive was verbally degrading myself. I would walk around all day telling myself how stupid I was and calling myself many bad names and telling myself over and over how I hated myself. It soon became evident I had to quit that sort of thing. It was like one day, "OK now, you can start living again. You've punished yourself long enough." Also, I came to realize my kids didn't deserve to live this way.
>
> I still have depressing times, but it seems now I can handle them better and when I'm in the process of living day by day, I can't dwell on the past so easily.[8]

Both figures of speech for depression, the dark night of the soul and the deep river, illustrate the fact that most people do not snap into depression, nor snap out of it. The "dark night" is preceded by dusk, a time of deepening shadows, and followed by dawn, when things become *gradually* brighter. The "deep river" usually has an approach which gradually descends, although there may be an event that causes a more sudden "drop-off," and the other side of the river is usually attained with the feeling that "I'm not over my head anymore; the current is still there, but the ground is getting higher, and I'm going to make it."

A card from Ann came about a year later.

> Just a note to let you know all is well here.
> Looking forward to this summer, compared to last.
> Good to be alive! Usual activity, always keeping busy.
> Also, Vacation Bible School this week, and so much more enjoyable than last year.[9]

The previous summer, as mentioned above, Ann had volunteered to help in Vacation Bible School even though she didn't "feel" like it. This year, the joy came. Ann had demonstrated the importance of taking action.

## Questions

1. Do you put yourself down by calling yourself names, such as "stupid"? If so, how has this helped you? Can you choose to stop this name-calling?
2. At those times when you are inactive because you are feeling down or depressed, what steps do you take to get moving again?
3. When you are feeling very sad, what steps do you take to help you *feel* better?

# CHAPTER THIRTEEN: TAKING ACTION

Suppose you are coming home from a meeting tonight. As you approach your house you notice that there are no lights on. You find your key, open the screen or storm door, and finally unlock the front door and go inside. You reach for the light switch in the hall and can't find it. You then discover, by feeling on the walls where the light switches should be in the hall, living room, and kitchen, that the switches are missing.

This search for the "light switch" is no fantasy for the depressed person. Things look gloomy and black. He tries to switch on good feelings—a zest for life, happiness, enthusiasm—but he can't find the switch. He may begin to panic as he desperately tries to find the answer to the question, "What can I do in order to *feel* better?"

Three of the symptoms given in the last chapter for depression were sadness, inactivity, and self-depreciation. Most depressed persons work on the first of these three symptoms: they try to feel better. This seems logical. If they felt better then they could start doing things again and this would solve the predicament of inactivity. Also, if they felt better they would not feel the need to put themselves down. Although it *seems* logical that a person who is feeling depressed would work at trying to feel better, this approach seldom works. Most people, particularly depressed persons, cannot find the switch to elevate their moods.

Let's suppose you are feeling depressed. You may just be quite discouraged or you may actually have the above symptoms of depression. Your mood may even be depressed deep enough and long enough that you identified with Ann in the last chapter. What steps can you take to make the journey back to health as rapid as possible? I suggest the following three steps. You need to understand that, like any suggestions one person makes to another, they work some of the time for some people.

These steps are: 1) Don't waste your energy trying to *feel* better; 2) Work at changing the way you are *doing* things; and 3) Start building yourself up instead of putting yourself down.

## Don't Try to Feel Better!

Cathy was a young woman in her middle twenties, married, with no children. She became involved in adultery with a fellow employee at the factory where she worked. After

# 147 : TAKING ACTION

several months she decided to end the relationship and tell her husband about it. Instead of becoming angry with her, he was able to tell her how deeply hurt he was and how it made him feel "like not much of a man." When Cathy later sought counseling to help to overcome her feelings of depression, she said she wished her husband had not been so nice. She would have felt better if he had been mean. Obviously she felt very guilty and believed that she needed to suffer more than she had for what she had done. However, she had asked for forgiveness from God as well as her husband. She said, "If I could just feel better. I'd give anything to wake up feeling good just one morning!"

I explained to Cathy that in an automobile accident where one has suffered injury, such as a broken leg, the body in a sense has been violated. We do not expect to feel better right away. We work rather at getting the leg cared for, being sure that we get rest generally, and making sure we do not put pressure on the injured part. In a similar way, when we violate our conscience, we cannot expect to feel good right away. We take the first step of confession and then, as much as possible, we make it right. But we may expect to feel bad for awhile. This simply shows that our conscience and our integrity are working. Later, the joy will gradually return.

There are other causes of depression than violating our conscience. But whatever the cause or causes of the depression, you will find it helpful to accept the reality that you usually won't find the switch to elevate your feelings right away. Assure yourself that the time will come when you *will* actually experience the emotions of joy, pleasure, and excitement. In the meantime, feeling down, although not a pleasant experience, is not necessarily a dreadful one either—unless you make it so. It may actually be a relief to realize that feeling better does not have to be your number one goal in life. Goals that are more important have to do with the way you are interacting with others, and how productive you are in your daily tasks. You may say, "I can't think about these things when I feel so bad." Another way to look at it is that you could if you *chose* to. The good news here is that you choose to do what you need to do rather than to be controlled by your feelings.

## Change the Way You Are Doing Things

It is easier to find the switch to change or control our actions than it is to find the switch that makes us feel better. Behavior is much easier to work with than feelings, because behavior is something we can see and something that is specific and concrete. What behaviors do you want to change? Depressed counselees that I have worked with, who were desperately trying to change the way they were doing things, have asked some very difficult questions. The questions that were most asked include those given below. Actually most of the answers to these questions came from the counselees themselves as they moved into action.

HOW DO I FACE THE MORNING?
Most of us find it difficult to get out of bed in the morning. The depressed person finds it much more difficult. Some wait until the rest of the family have left the house and then get up. Some go back to sleep until the middle of the morning or until noon and then get up. At any rate facing the morning is a major task for most depressed persons.

To face east one looks one direction, to face west one looks another direction, and to face the morning one needs to look up. How then does one look up? One way to do this is with music. Several persons who have made the journey from depression back to health have said that music in the morning has helped. One volunteer service is based on this idea. Ralph Hoy in 1957 began a service called "Recordings for Recovery."[1] This is a nonprofit organization which provides musical tapes without charge to hospitals, prisons, and individuals. Some of the world's top musical talent is used in this venture. You can use the same approach. After you find your way to the alarm clock and turn it off, move on to your stereo or tape deck and get a more pleasant sound going.

Another way to look up is to begin talking with your husband or wife. This, of course, requires some commitment and cooperation on the part of the other person. If your spouse is not a "morning person," or if you live alone, you can still use the talking approach. A number of people have made arrangements with friends so they can call them when they need to, even in the morning. It is important to keep these morning calls brief so the other person doesn't have to rush to get caught up.

An activity many have successfully used to look up at the beginning of the day is to say a Bible verse several times to oneself or aloud. My own favorite verse to say is, "Serve the Lord with gladness! Come into his presence with singing!" (Psalm 100:2). Then after I get dressed, I often take my old $17.95 guitar and sing a few songs, such as "Let's Just Praise the Lord," or "Morning Has Broken." The noise I generate by doing this has a fringe benefit—it usually wakes the rest of the family up. (I suppose I should think more about whether it helps them start their day in a positive way or not!) You don't have to be able to play a musical instrument or even feel like singing in order to sing. You just have to *decide* to do it. You may find, as I have, that you *feel* more like singing after you have sung than before you started.

## 150 : DEPRESSION

Some like to read the morning paper while they drink a cup of coffee. I usually read the paper for information, but it doesn't do much (except sometimes for the comic strip "Peanuts") to help me look up in the morning. Reading Scripture or a devotional book helps. For those who don't like to read first thing in the morning, you may wish to listen to Bible portions commercially available on cassettes, or you can tape your own.

You may have noticed by the above suggestions that the processes of input and output are *both* necessary to look up at the beginning of the day, just as inhaling and exhaling are necessary to life. We take in by reading or listening. We express ourselves by talking (including prayer) or singing.

After you have faced the morning by looking up through these means, you still have to find strength for the many tasks you have to do. This need brings us to the next question.

HOW DO I FIND THE ENERGY TO BEGIN MY WORK DAY?
Another way to phrase that question is, "How am I presently wasting my energy?" The concept behind this second question is that it is possible for us to have energy leaks. If we have inner tensions that are working against each other, this creates an energy leak. If we have too many of these leaks, then all our surplus energy is wasted.

Suppose that a person is depressed and she thinks, "I have seven loads of washing I need to do, I need to go grocery shopping, I should go and see my aunt, and I promised Jimmy that I would take him to the library." Now suppose she just worries about all the work she has to do, without organizing these tasks in some kind of priority list. This creates an energy leak.

The first step in plugging such leaks is to separate what it is you *want* to do from what you *need* to do. Usually persons who

## 151 : TAKING ACTION

are depressed have been living pretty much by what they want to do and this has immersed them deeper and deeper in their predicament. Once you have established what it is you need to do, then pick from this list of activities one thing to do. If you can't decide which is the most important out of the top two things that need doing, toss a coin. It will be much easier to find energy for your work day after you have centered on one specific task.

MEANING IN LIFE

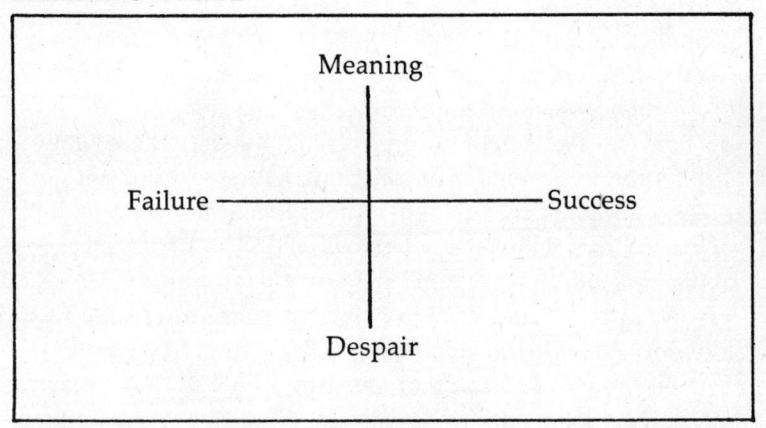

```
                    Meaning
                       |
                       |
       Failure ————————+———————— Success
                       |
                       |
                    Despair
```

(From Victor E. Frankl)[2]

Sometimes another source of strength is to reflect on what has meaning in your life. You may respond, "That's why I'm depressed. Nothing in my life has any meaning." But could it be that at this point you are responding to your feelings and general emotional outlook, rather than to those parts of your life that you *know* have meaning, whether you feel like it or not right now? You may feel like a failure, but as Victor Frankl has shown, meaning in life is not dependent on being successful. One can have failed many times and still find a great deal of meaning in life. The diagram "Meaning in Life" illustrates Frankl's view of the relationship of failure and success to despair and meaning.

If our meaning in life comes from being successful in all our efforts each day, then our feelings and energy will be like a yo-yo. The number and extent of the ups and downs will depend on the amount and degree of our successes and failures. Frankl's view is helpful here because he shows that meaning in life is on a vertical dimension rather than a horizontal dimension.

Shelley said she had been depressed "for a long time." She felt like a failure as a mother. When she began keeping track of what she was doing and not doing as a mother, she decided her feelings of failure were legitimate. She actually *was* failing in a number of functions. Often she did not get breakfast for her children. Sometimes they went to school with dirty clothes because she failed to do the washing. In talking about this she said, "I don't get any meaning from preparing meals and washing clothes. Those things are just like doing the dishes; it's the same old thing every day." It was becoming apparent that meaning in life for her involved more than just caring for her family. When she was asked the question, "What would have a great deal of meaning for you?" she replied that she had been wanting for some time to "help the elderly." Her own grandmother had been very important to her, and now her grandmother was no longer living. "But there are so many older persons, I wouldn't know where to start." In response to the question, "Who is the one older person you'd like most to reach out to?" she said that it would be the neighbor woman living alone whom she had been planning to visit for a long time, but she couldn't "find the time." Shelley made a commitment to visit her neighbor once a week for a month just as a friend, not as a "helper." One of the reasons she had not gone over to visit her sooner was that deep inside, she knew it wasn't quite right to visit other persons just to help them. It is somewhat condescending, in the same way that some foreign aid programs may be condescending. (A little nation may not accept a handout from a large nation.) But the idea of visiting her as a friend freed her from the notion that she should go across the street and do something for that lady. At the end of a month, Shelley was functioning somewhat better with her family and was feeling better. She had found that her new friend was a good listener and that she was receiving as much help as she was giving. Finding meaning in life through reaching outside her own family enabled Shelley to meet her own family's needs more effectively.

IS MEDICATION NECESSARY?
This is another question that is frequently asked by persons suffering from depression. The severely depressed person may find medication helpful for a time in facing the day and finding energy to work. This medication should be prescribed by a psychiatrist, or by another physician in conjunction with a psychologist. There are two points of view that are helpful concerning medication: 1) The fact that I need to take medication until I can learn to elevate my own moods does not mean I am a bad person. 2) Taking medication will not make me permanently better. Medication for depression is probably neither as bad as it has been pictured by some, nor as good as it has been pictured by others. A helpful point of view in taking any mood-altering drug is to get off it as soon as possible. Any drug has some kind of trade-off; that is, it may help one part of the organism, and upset some other part. At any rate, one's goal

should be to become a fully-functioning person who is not dependent on any chemical to elevate his moods.

## HOW CAN I GET OVER MY FEAR OF CROWDS?
Many depressed persons panic when they think about going to a restaurant, to the supermarket or to church. This condition, agoraphobia (the fear of crowded places), is fairly common among anxious persons as well as those suffering from depression. Among the fears that dart through the consciousness are: "I may get dizzy or pass out," "It's getting hard to breathe," "What will people think when they notice my funny breathing?" "My family will be embarrassed if they have to take me out right in the middle of the meal (or the church service)."

Often it helps just to know these fears are not so unusual. Many persons have successfully learned to free themselves from the predicament of a particular phobia by moving towards it in small steps. To use this method to overcome the fear of crowded places, one first thinks himself through the situation. You "see" yourself being asked by your husband to eat out, and responding "Yes." Then you imagine yourself getting ready, driving to the restaurant, getting out of the car, walking into the restaurant, ordering—going through every step. Then you actually go to a restaurant, a small one at first when it isn't very busy. Later you go to larger ones at peak times. Sitting at a table that is close to a rest room helps you to know that you can leave without walking in front of many other people.

Another method of dealing with fear is one that Bruce Larson describes in his practical book *Living on the Growing Edge*.[3] He suggests the way to overcome fear is to walk directly into it, and quotes the saying, "Do the thing you fear most and the death of fear is certain."[4] Those who have found the courage to implement this method have found that it also works.

## Building Yourself Up

One of the symptoms of depression is putting one's self down. Now it is not enough to simply try to *stop* putting one's self down. One cannot build a new, positive life style by stopping anything. Jesus illustrated this by telling the story of a man who swept his house after one unclean spirit left, only to discover later that the unclean spirit moved back in with seven other, more evil spirits.[5] The man erred, in that although the house was swept and in order, he left it empty. In the same way there must be a *positive* force if the depression is to be lifted.

Such a force can be found in the second greatest commandment, "You shall love your neighbor as yourself." The implication here is that we love ourselves and it is all right to do so. It is nothing we have to be taught to do. This love comes as original equipment. It doesn't mean that we always have a warm, positive feeling about ourselves. The depressed person doesn't even like himself, let alone have the kinds of emotions toward himself that we would typically call love. To love ourselves means that we desire good for ourselves. Perhaps even the suicide believes he is doing himself a favor.

Although we do not have to be taught *to* love ourselves, most of us can profit by learning *how to* love ourselves in ways that will build us up (not puff us up). Perhaps the ways we are to love God can serve as a model for loving ourselves and others. Jesus said, when asked what commandment was the most important, "The first is, 'Hear, O Israel: the Lord our God, the Lord is one; and you shall love the Lord your God with all your heart, and with all your soul, and with all your mind, and with all your strength' " (Mark 12:29, 30). Now obviously, we are not to love ourselves or our neighbors with *all* our heart, soul, etc. But if we reserve the "all" for our relationship to God, then we may safely look on the four ways of loving (heart, soul, mind, and strength) as valid for relating to ourselves and others, as well as relating to God. Some scholars have said that these are just words piled on each other to show that we are to love God with our whole being. However, it seems more valid to believe that Jesus attached specific meanings to the words that he quoted and used.

The chart, "Ways of Loving," shows the four ways of loving, and provides a definition for each of these terms. The third column then shows each term as having to do with a channel of loving. If you can visualize a river with four channels leading into it, think of the flow of the river as being the totality of our love to God, others, or ourselves, with the channels being the ways, or processes, by which we love.

WAYS OF LOVING

| Term | Meaning | Channel |
|---|---|---|
| Heart | Innermost self, no pretense, sincerely, our whole being is in agreement, centered on one object which is valued or chosen | Choosing |
| Soul | Seat of emotions, feelings | Feeling |
| Mind | Understanding, thinking | Thinking |
| Strength | Force, ability, might, using one's energy, gathering all one's resources for action | Doing |

We are to love with our *hearts*. This has to do with valuing, or choosing, the person with no reservations. The depressed person may say, "I can't love myself." A more accurate statement would be, "Although I love myself, I'm choosing to treat myself badly." The basis for choosing to treat oneself better is that God loves us and chooses to nourish and cherish us.

> *Believe it,*
> *You are a real find,*
> *A joy in someone's heart.*
> *You're a jewel,*
> *Unique and priceless.*
> *I don't care how you feel.*
> *Believe it,*
> *God don't make no junk.*[6]

This verse emphasizes we are worthwhile, whether we feel like it or not, because we are created in the image of God.

The second way we are to love is with our *souls*. The channel involved here is feeling. The relationship can be illustrated by referring to "soul music," music which expresses a great deal of feeling. Loving ourselves with our souls would indicate we are to open ourselves up to experiencing warm feelings about ourselves. The depressed person cannot *make* himself get warm emotional vibrations toward himself, but he can welcome such feelings, rather than reject them, when they do come.

We are also to love ourselves with our *minds*. It is important for the depressed person to put his mind back in gear and to straighten out his thoughts. Many persons inwardly make such statements as "I'll never get better," "Everything is hopeless," or "There is nothing I can do." If we straighten our communication out, we will begin to drop such words from our thinking as "never," "hopeless," or "nothing," in terms of making predictions about our future.

We are to love ourselves with our *strength*. The other ways we are to love ourselves include choosing, feeling, and thinking. This final way, the way of strength, emphasizes doing, that is, action. The depressed person loves himself in this way when he gets out of bed in the morning so that he can get his work done. He expresses his love to himself when he nourishes his body by eating what is necessary to keep his energy up. He uses every last bit of strength to do what he knows he needs to do.

In addition to opening new channels to love ourselves and beginning to take action again, another helpful step is to reach out to other persons who are immersed in a predicament and help them move out of it.

## Only Scarred Hands Heal

Do you buy the statement that "only scarred hands heal?" The concept behind this phrase is that we must have come through a predicament which was so serious that we realized that "cheap" advice and pat answers don't work. In other words we have experienced for ourselves the difference between a problem, in which advice is helpful, and a predicament, in which it is not. Having experienced this, we will not give easy answers to the person we are trying to help.

I think it is true that "only scarred hands heal." However, I don't believe that we have to have experienced the *same* scar as another person in order to be with him in a helpful way. Having come through a deep predicament ourselves, we understand that it is far more healing to come with a listening attitude than with a fast "solution."

Ann, the woman whose journey back to health from depression was described in the last chapter, began to reach out to another person just as soon as she found the strength

# 159 : TAKING ACTION

to do it. It happened that the person whom Ann reached out to was suffering from depression just as Ann had been. Ann invested herself in being with her friend when she needed her and in doing things with her. As a result her friend gained healing and strength, and Ann herself grew stronger from the experience.

## Questions

1. How do you begin your day? Is this way of starting the day working for you?
2. Is your meaning in life dependent on how successful you are?
3. I asked earlier whether you agreed with the statement, "Only scarred hands heal." If you do, and if you have some scars, to whom will you reach out in a helping, healing way?

# CHAPTER FOURTEEN: THE GIFT OF INVOLVEMENT

In the previous chapter I offered some suggestions concerning how the depressed person could help himself. In this chapter let's look at some ways other family members can help the depressed person move out of this particular predicament. Among the questions posed by family members about a depressed spouse, child, parent, or sibling, the following occur most frequently: How do I get them up? How can I get them started working? They always seem interested in themselves; how can I get them interested in others? How can I get them out of the house to go see some friends or to go shopping or go to a restaurant? How can I

## 161 : THE GIFT OF INVOLVEMENT

get them motivated to *want* to do something?

The concept of motivation ties all of the above questions together. Motivation offers a great deal of potential. There are Motivation Seminars, Motivation Workshops, as well as a number of Motivation Institutes springing up around the country. However, motivation is not living up to its promising potential. People are "motivated," there is a resulting flare-up of action, and then the flame dies out. Motivation is an intangible, abstract term. The concept of *involvement* offers more direction and potential for change than does motivation. In discussing these two concepts, Dr. William Glasser has said that they are similar except that involvement is something that can be done directly and motivation is not.[1] Involvement is important, says Glasser, because it works against loneliness. Certainly people suffering from depression are acutely aware of their loneliness.

Sarah Fraser has described the lonely journey of a person in a period of depression as follows:

> During a depression one is swathed in apathy. Nothing seems edible. Because of inability to eat, I lose eight or ten pounds with each bout. Everything is negative; there is no joy to be found in family, friends, music, TV, work, nature, reading, exercise, church, or whatever else might give happiness in better days. I have been an avid collector, but when girded in the glums, I literally shake about these treasures. I see how I have burdened our lives with things, whether by my own doing or by inheritance. But I am far enough along this lonesome trail now to know that there will be an "up" time again when these items may hold beauty for me afresh.[2]

The "trail" may be different in several respects for others suffering from depression, but the "lonesome" aspect of the journey seems to be true for all. Therefore, the biggest gift we can give a family member suffering from depression is our involvement. However, usually exactly the opposite happens. The depressed person is no fun to be with so family members tend to move away from rather than toward him. They tend to do things without that family member rather than with him. Sometimes, family members misunderstand the nature of the depressed person's condition and are ashamed of him. They may in this situation pretend that person does not exist. Many family members who are not ashamed and who decide to help the depressed person even though it is sometimes not a pleasant thing to do are faced with another difficulty—being made to feel helpless. The person suffering from depression feels hopeless and helpless. The helper who is trying to intervene with such a person nearly always picks up some of these helpless feelings. Then, believing that he is unable to make a difference, he backs off and leaves the person totally alone.

## Securing Involvement

The word "involve" means "to draw in as a participant."[3] To involve someone means that we must take the initiative in terms of drawing them into an activity in which they will become not a spectator, but a participant. It is important that this activity not just be something to get the person "busy," but that it be an activity that needs to be done. Most people learn to recognize and back off from busy work at an early age.

An important question to ask oneself is, "Am *I* willing to get involved?" If we are not willing to get involved, then we may give them advice, suggest they take a pill to make them feel better, or scold them. All of these may be used as methods to *avoid* involvement. If our answer to this question is that

## 163 : THE GIFT OF INVOLVEMENT

we *are* willing to become involved, then instead of trying to do something *for* them (or *to* them), we will try to do some things *with* them.

Involvement means you sometimes help the depressed family member in getting up. Conversation may help. When an airport is "socked in" with darkness and fog, traffic control may "talk" the airliner down for a landing. When a person is depressed and can't "see out" very well, they may need to be talked up. Or you may put one of their favorite records on the stereo.

To get them to "do something," whether it is working or shopping or visiting, you may need to do this with them. Remember, they feel very lonely. Sometimes they won't go, and that's all right. The important thing is, "Don't give up." Sometimes they may get angry with you. For some depressed persons, this is a sign of growth. They have had all their anger turned in on themselves. Beginning to focus some of it on a loved one may be the first step in getting rid of it. Work hard at not being intimidated nor made angry by their anger. Maintain the involvement. It will be one of the hardest things you have ever done. But later you will be glad you gave this gift of forbearance, time, and energy.

It is difficult, but possible, to remain calm when another family member gets "mad." I awoke one morning feeling abused, tired, and discouraged for some reason. I believe now that I was looking at all of the things I had to do that day. (What tires me the most is not doing things but thinking about them.) At any rate I didn't like anything about myself that morning, and I particularly didn't like my grouchiness. This made me even grouchier. After breakfast, while the children were getting ready for school, Lillian asked me a question about our budget. I don't remember the question now; I think I've repressed it. But it was a perfectly reasonable question. However, at that time I didn't want to talk about money or anything. So I shot back the answer, "I don't know." Given the inflection of my voice, this answer (translated) came out, "I don't care. Just leave me alone." Lillian did not get angry, nor was she intimidated by my sulkiness and anger. She just dropped the subject because it was clear we weren't going to make any progress on the issue. I went off to work feeling miserable. I always feel lousy whenever I mistreat someone, especially someone I love. In the middle of the morning I called Lillian from my office and apologized to her for my grumpiness. Then I began to feel better. The fact that she didn't attack me or back off from me when I was surly helped me to deal with where I was and what I needed to do about it.

There are several other guidelines which may be helpful in getting involved with a family member who is suffering from depression:

1. *Realize it is a family predicament.* Sometimes the rest of the family views the predicament as being only that of the depressed member. Actually it is a *family* predicament. It occurred in a family setting and it is best treated in the family setting. This differs from other situations where help is needed. For example, if a car needs a tune-up, we take it to a garage to get that done. If a child breaks an arm, we take him to the hospital to get it set. But if persons are suffering from depression, they can't be sent out to get it "fixed" and then brought back with the anticipation that everything will be all right. The trend now is to treat the individual person suffering from depression while the person remains in the community and in the home. If hospitalization is required, an effort is made to keep it a month or less rather than one that would last several months or maybe even a year.

If the depressed person leaves the home and is hospitalized

for a long period of time, there is a tendency for the family to close up and, without meaning to, make the family member's reentry into the family extremely difficult. Those families who have had children leave for college and come back for the summer realize that no matter how much love is there, some readjustment is necessary on the part of the individual and the rest of the family.

2. *Don't be discouraged if the involvement process takes awhile.* We need to understand that our efforts to get involved may not be welcomed at first. When I was a boy I nearly drowned in a Kansas farm pond, but an older neighbor boy pulled me out despite my thrashing around and generally uncooperative behavior. I desperately needed his involvement but was unable to welcome it at the time. The lonely person, like the drowning person, needs help but may resist it. So, be willing to be rebuffed by the lonely, depressed person, and not take the rebuff personally.

3. *Do not label the depressed person as mentally ill.* Labeling persons is a way in which we separate ourselves from them, become detached from them, and become uninvolved with them. Langsley and Kaplan in their excellent book, *The Treatment of Families in Crisis*, discuss what happens when a family appends this label to one of its members.

> When a family decides that they have a "mentally ill" person in the home, certain common assumptions are made. The label signifies the existence of a mysterious, frightening, long-term disorder. The usual connotations are that the patient is no longer responsible for his behavior or for carrying on normal responsibilities of living in a family.[4]

Such labeling causes an unnecessary crisis in the home. Most of this crisis stems from the power of expectation, mentioned above. If the depressed person is regarded as frightening, he becomes frightened of himself; if he is regarded as not being responsible, he becomes irresponsible; and if he is seen as "different," he feels set apart, isolated, and lonely.

4. *Adopt this point of view toward the depressed family member: "We need you."* Military psychiatrists and psychologists have noted how important it is in recovery for the emotionally disturbed person to feel needed.[5] In the early stages of World War II and the Korean episode when we had enough men, they were sent back to the U.S. or at least far away from the front lines to recuperate. The message, though implicit, was quite clear: "We expect it will take you a long time to get well, and we can get along without you." When we began to run out of men, and when it was found that the period of recuperation was usually lengthy, a new system was started. The treatment was carried out in the rear lines, not far from the soldier's own unit. These men got the message, "We expect you to get well fast because we need you." These wartime experiences confirmed the old observation about human nature that usually people do what they are expected to do.

It is important, then, to let the person suffering from depression know that we need him. This must be a genuine point of view rather than just an idea that we are trying to get across to the other person. If we tell that person we need him but continue to do his work over a long period of time, he gets the real message that we can get along without him. The depressed person needs a short time of rest and relaxation, but he should be involved again as rapidly as possible in the ongoing work of the family.

The above guidelines center on the importance of the gift of involvement. It turns out to be giving yourself. Every meeting of persons is an exchange of gifts. To really "meet" the

## 167 : THE GIFT OF INVOLVEMENT

depressed person requires a great energy and time investment on your part.

## Questions
1. Have you built an involvement with a depressed person? Would you like to, using the guidelines given in this chapter? Be prepared for it to take some strength out of you.

# five: the struggle for independence

*As the children get older, separation and the thought of it may cause both anxiety and anger.*

# CHAPTER FIFTEEN: THREATENED BY THE STRUGGLE

I make it a point to listen to the songs youth listen to, because many of the songs have a worthwhile message, and because the themes of the songs help me understand the issues with which young people are concerned. One of the recurring themes of songs in the "Top Forty" is the struggle for independence in which many youth are involved. Two songs which have been popular in the past describe situations in which this struggle has become intense.

"She's Leaving Home," a Lennon-McCartney song, tells about the *anxiety* a girl has as she runs away from home.

## 172 : THE STRUGGLE FOR INDEPENDENCE

She quietly leaves home early one morning—crying. In a sense she gains freedom, but she wishes she could have communicated better with her parents. When they discover she has gone, her parents wonder what they have done wrong. They feel they have invested much of their lives in her.

Another song, Cat Stevens's "Father and Son," is about the lack of communication between a father and son, and the resulting feelings of *anger* the son has.

> *How can I try to explain,*
> *cause when I do*
> *he turns away again.*
> *It's always been the same,*
> *the same old story.*
> *From the moment I could talk*
> *I was ordered to listen;*
> *now there's a way*
> *and I know that I have to go.*
> *Away,*
> *I know I have to go.*[1]

Probably in most families the struggle is not so intense, nor the feelings so harsh as those sung about here. Nevertheless, in nearly all families the struggle does occur and the two feelings described in these songs—anxiety and anger—cause many predicaments. The effects of anxiety and anger are more easily understood by persons observing a family from the outside than by the family members. Have you seen a family where there was so much tension generated by this struggle that the family "came apart at the seams" with anxiety and could no longer hold the young person (who may not have been "ready" for a separate life)? Or have you observed a situation in which a family explodes with anger and propels the young person out of the home, regardless of his or her ability to make it alone? If you have seen these particular family predicaments, you understand the dynamic energy that can be unleashed in a destructive way.

## Separation: a Cause of Anxiety and Anger in the Struggle for Independence

Infants are born with several fears that come as original equipment. One of these is the fear of loud sounds, another is the fear of being dropped, and a third is the fear of abandonment. This fear of abandonment, the fear of being separated from loved ones, gradually becomes the emotion of loneliness in youth and adults.

This fear of separation, a part of all of us, becomes terrifying in some. I remember one senior in high school who could not concentrate on his studies because he didn't know who he was. His identity predicament was greater than most of us have had, because as a child and adolescent, he had been switched back and forth between his mother and stepfather and his father and stepmother so many times that he had lost track of the number. He would stay in one home as long as they could stand him and he could stand them, and then he would be rotated to the other home. During much of his early childhood he had been unsure of his last name because one set of parents had insisted that he be called by their last name even though it was not his legal last name. By the time he was in high school he knew what his legal last name was, but he was not sure he wanted it. It is easy to see why school work was not the most important thing to him, given his emptiness and his lack of a sense of belonging. The early and frequent switching of mothers probably contributed to this lack. It appears extremely important for most infants and young children to have an early, solid, warm experience with their mother.

John Bowlby is probably the leading world authority on maternal deprivation, the situation in which a child is separated from his or her mother for a significant length of time during the infancy or preschool period. He says that past separation or impending separation can frustrate the child to such an extent that he becomes either anxious or angry or both.[2] Now we would anticipate that a child under this condition would become anxious. But the idea of anger being a result catches our attention. Yet there is enough in our own observations that this has a ring of truth. For example in bereavement (separation by death) most persons have observed anger at least in some situations. Sometimes this anger is turned on the mortician, the minister, or some other person helping with the funeral, and centers upon such little details that it is apparent the real anger is directed elsewhere and simply comes out on a "safe" person. In divorce (separation by choice) both anxiety and anger are expressed. School phobia (fear of school) and agoraphobia (fear of crowded places) may often be traced to anxiety caused by separation. Agoraphobia is a condition that has received a considerable amount of attention, especially in the last five years, and is frequently observed, as mentioned earlier, among persons who are depressed and anxious.

Bowlby wisely calls attention to the fact that anxiety and anger come from the same root word.[3] An illustration of the closeness of these conditions may be seen by observing wild animals. Their reactions to the approach of a human being are of a flight-fight nature (anxiety-anger). If they can get away, they take flight. On the other hand, you may have seen animals, either in real life or on TV, which if cornered and separated from their "family" and safety, will often fight.

# 175 : THREATENED BY THE STRUGGLE

Therefore, whether the animal fights or takes flight depends not so much on the animal as on the person approaching it.

This simple observation offers an important guideline for families in which the children are becoming adolescents. If the parents and teenagers work with each other in a way which does not threaten and "corner" the others, the chance that anger and aggressiveness will be expressed will be considerably reduced.

## A FAMILY PREDICAMENT

As parents you want your children to get to the place where they don't need you any more, but you're anxious about the separation you know is coming. Your children want to become independent, but they, too, are anxious about the impending separation. If all are aware of the dynamics of this situation, they will be more patient with the other family members.

The separation will have happy as well as unhappy outcomes. Otto Rank has written about the trauma of separation caused by birth. It is his theory that birth trauma is so great that its consequences are felt throughout life. Another way to look at it is that the trauma would be greater if the baby were not born. The same can be said for the adolescent. The anxiety caused by the separation when the child chooses to leave home is always there. On the other hand if the child remains dependent and makes the choice to remain home all his life, the anxiety could be greater for both the child and his parents.

## CONFLICT RESOLUTION

The families that work effectively with predicaments are those that do not back off from them. Nearly all conflicts can be resolved if people approach them with the point of view that they can be worked out.

## 176 : THE STRUGGLE FOR INDEPENDENCE

Peggy felt she couldn't wait to graduate from high school and go away to college because she and her parents "were always yelling at each other." But in November of her freshman year in college she found she was missing them a great deal. She felt she would be able to concentrate on her college courses better if she and her parents could resolve their conflict. Peggy finally decided to go home during Thanksgiving vacation and "have it out." But she was afraid she would fail—that they wouldn't listen to her. She dropped in to see me before she left on vacation and asked how to go about talking with her parents. I suggested she:

1. Start with one thing she appreciated, then move to the disagreement that was separating them. The issue that started the rift was that she believed her parents let her brothers have a great deal more freedom than they had permitted her. Her first statement therefore could be, "I appreciate the fact that you love me and you have wanted to protect me." This statement would let her parents know that she valued their love and that she knew that they were trying to do the best for her they could.

2. Listen to her parents as intently as she wanted them to listen to her.

3. Keep her voice volume low and her rate fairly slow. As much as possible she should avoid having an edge on her voice.

4. Practice deep breathing if she began to get scared or angry.

Peggy saw me the following Monday and reported that it had been a difficult weekend, but that she had not backed off from the confrontation with her parents. They had not fully gotten together yet but most of her bitter feelings were gone. And she and her parents were going to continue the dialogue at Christmas time. The biggest factor in her favor had been that

## 177 : THREATENED BY THE STRUGGLE

she went into the weekend determined to resolve the conflict.

I enjoy reading bumper stickers. In Kearney, Nebraska, where I live, the bumper sticker promoted by our Chamber of Commerce is KEARNEY: CAN DO COUNTRY. Usually bumper stickers are to bring about a condition rather than to state one. However, according to Nebraska historian Dr. Robert Manley, Kearney has a history of being a community with a "boomer mentality."[4] In the late 1880s, for example, some of the people who lived in Kearney saw no limit as to its growth. One person called for the capital of the United States to be moved to Kearney, and others said this would be the new Chicago of the West because the main line tracks of the Union Pacific met the Burlington Railway tracks near Kearney. And in 1889, only a few years after Edison had invented the electric light bulb, Kearney had electric lights, also a streetcar system, a brick factory, and a cotton mill—all powered by electricity. Of these four innovations, only the electric lights survived the early nineteen hundreds. However, the roots of a community, like the roots of a person, influence what is going on currently. And Kearney is at it again. It has grown by 50 percent in the last ten years and many of the citizens feel "the sky is the limit."

The "can do" point of view has some problems but it has many advantages. If a community or a family looks out at the world and in at itself with a "can do" philosophy, progress is more likely to be made and conflicts are more likely to be resolved. It is particularly important for a family in which there are teenagers and parents who will soon be separated, to have a "can do" point of view. With this positive point of view they will find that 1 Corinthians 10:13 is correct, "No temptation has overtaken you that is not common to man. God is faithful, and he will not let you be tempted beyond your strength, but with the temptation will also provide the way of escape, that you may be able to endure it." Even the temptation to be anxious and angry at the thought of impending separation from loved ones will lose its power as the family members realize that this is a common situation to everyone and that it is one that can be worked out.

In the community in which I grew up there was a woman about sixty-five who had a forty-year-old son who lived with her. They were referred to as Mrs. Blank and her boy. This sometimes occurs where the dependency needs of the child or the parent is very great and these needs are not resolved. It needs to be pointed out, though, that some children continue on into adulthood living with their parents, in order to take care of them or because they did not choose to marry or for some other reason that would not necessarily indicate a dependency relationship.

COMMON TO ALL
The condition of separation that causes anxiety and anger is common to all families. It occurred even in the family of Jesus. At the age of twelve when Jesus and his family went up to Jerusalem for the feast of the Passover, he stayed in Jerusalem with the teachers while Mary and Joseph began the trip home. When they came back and found him, Mary's statement showed both anxiety and anger: "Son, why have you treated us so? Behold, your father and I have been looking for you anxiously" (Luke 2:48). At the age of twelve, Jesus, like other Jewish boys, had obtained a new measure of independence. Mary was probably reacting to that and the impending separation she knew was approaching, as well as the actual separation of the moment.

Sometimes you who are parents may feel, "Why are we the only ones who have the troubles we do with children who don't want to be bossed?" And your children may be

## THREATENED BY THE STRUGGLE

reflecting on the question, "Why aren't my parents willing to trust me?" It helps both parents and children when they realize this is a situation common to other families as well as theirs. This realization greatly reduces the amount of anger and anxiety present in the family.

## Questions

1. Have you listened this week to some of the songs your children or teenagers are listening to? What are the themes (main ideas) of these songs?
2. Has there been anxiety or anger expressed in your family this week? Can you connect these expressions to separation or impending separation?
3. Do you back off from family conflicts started by anxiety or anger, or do you take a "can do" approach to resolving such conflicts?

# CHAPTER SIXTEEN: IT'S HARD TO LET GO!

As human beings we don't have to learn to grasp; we do have to learn to let go. When the palm of a newborn baby is stimulated, he instinctively reacts by taking a grip on the finger or object used to stimulate him. Some babies grip so tightly that they can hang by their hands for as long as a minute.[1] Observers have found that "voluntary grasping supplants reflex grasping at about age four months, but even then, once the baby has something in his hand, the still-persistent grasp reflex makes it impossible for him to let go."[2] The striking thing about this observation is that the infant *cannot* let go.

We noticed this grasp reflex with our own children when they were babies. Then when they got to the six- to nine-month stage, we observed them embarking on the delightful adventure (to them) of letting things go. They would sit near the edge of the crib, or stand with support, and drop their rattle or other objects over the edge of the crib onto the floor. It seemed like a game to us as parents (and it soon developed into one) in which the baby dropped a toy and we picked it up only to see it dropped again. But at first it was not a game but rather an exploration of how it feels to let go and see an object separate from oneself. At this point the baby had *learned* to let go.

Most parents go through the same two stages the infant does—at first we grasp and then we learn to let go. Parents don't have to learn to take a newborn baby and hold it close to them. They instinctively love what they have helped to create. And the source of this love is not difficult to trace. God loves what he has created ("And God saw everything that he had made, and behold, it was very good," Genesis 1:31). Since we have been created in the image of God, we also love what we have had a part in creating. So the parents love and hold on to their child without ever having *learned* to do that. Then there comes a time when the parent discovers that loving his or her child means letting go. And at this discovery many of us become anxious.

## Understanding Separation Anxiety

If parents understand that anxiety is a natural response to the approaching separation from their children, they are much more able to prepare for it and to deal with it when it comes. One way to prepare for it is to recognize that we cannot say "my child" in the same way that we say "my house" or "my clothes." We cannot *possess* our children. Even though God created us, he did not choose to possess us. Human beings are not made to be possessed. The concept of possessing people is a devilish ideal. Scripture often speaks of demon-possession.

A workable point of view for us has been that our children were entrusted to us. I remember that before our first child was born, Lillian copied down the injunction from Pharaoh's daughter to Moses's mother, "Take this child away, and nurse him for me, and I will give you your wages" (Exodus 2:9). We have seen our role to be a similar one—that of nurturing the children God gave to us as a trust. This has not made letting go an easy process, but I think it has made it more possible and has allowed us to see the letting-go process in perspective.

The instinctive reaction of parents who sense impending separation from their child is the same as the infant—a grasping reflex. Now when a teenager feels he is grasped too tightly he also has a reflex action! His reflex action is to do whatever he has to in order to get loose. It is possible that when we hold something (or someone) too tightly in our fist, it may squirt out or squirm to be free.

One of the most extreme cases of unresolved parental separation anxiety I've read about is the funny-tragic battle of a fifty-four-year-old mother and her adult son, reported by Mike Royko in his interesting *Chicago Daily News* column.[3] I'll retell it to you because extreme cases often show clearly the dynamics operating in ordinary situations.

This woman's son did not call her ("I'd drop dead from surprise if he ever phoned me.") so she called him—thirty to forty times a day according to his count. This caused enough problems at home and work that he had an injunction brought to stop her from telephoning him. After

130 more calls from her, according to his log, he had her jailed overnight ("There it was the Easter season. Some sons send flowers to their mothers; my son sends the sheriff.").

Her anxiety about his welfare and her belief that he was unsafe apart from her, were the reasons she would not let him go. These concerns surface in her statement, "I wouldn't put him in jail. He's so skinny, I'd be worrying that he wasn't getting enough to eat. He's always been so skinny."

Finally she describes what she believes the real problem is. "I'll tell you what it is. Kids are different, nowadays. They are very selfish. They just live for themselves. That's what the problem is."

She still saw her adult son as a "kid." Is it possible that *we* see our own children as younger and less able than they actually are? Besides the obvious characteristics of their age and grade in school, do we know their present height, weight, the skills they have in crafts or sports, their new interests which have emerged this year, and the way they see life differently than they did a year (or a month) ago? Do we know what units they are currently studying in their subjects in school? What their dreams are in life? The idea in the old song, "You Tell Me Your Dream, and I'll Tell You Mine," is one that has value in the interaction between parents and children.

## Controlling Separation Anxiety

We probably can't eliminate the anxiety caused by the approaching and actual separation from our loved ones as they grow up and leave home. The best we can hope for is to learn how to control it so it does not cause severe family predicaments.

Would you believe it if I told you that a key to controlling separation anxiety is talking? Listen to this: "Have no anxiety about anything, but in everything by prayer and supplication with thanksgiving let your requests be made known to God. And the peace of God which passes all understanding, will keep your hearts and your minds in Christ Jesus" (Philippians 4:6, 7). We are to talk to God and let him know what it is we want in our relationship with our children. He has entrusted them to us; now it's up to us to trust him for them as we begin to let them go.

Talking with God is generally valued because of its intercessory role. It is often undervalued or even overlooked as a way to reduce our anxiety. But this Bible passage in Philippians places relief from anxiety alongside talking to God. An additional idea of this passage is that we are not only to make our *requests* known as we talk with God, but we are also to make our *thanks* known. Requesting involves receiving, and thanking involves giving. Thus prayer becomes a two-way process which makes it a genuine dialogue.

As we talk with God and trust him for our children, we need to remember that letting them go is a process, not something we do all at once. I'm not arguing for permissiveness. As James Dobson has so effectively explained, the child who grows up in a structured setting with clear, high expectations feels better about himself and becomes a more competent person.[4] Letting our children go little by little requires us to know them and their capabilities very well, and then to trust them.

One mother called to say she had a problem because her 16-year-old girl now had "wheels" (she had just gotten her driver's license). The mother was concerned because "I can't trust my daughter; I don't think she's telling me the truth." As the mother continued talking, she said the trust between the two of them had begun to diminish several years earlier. She had many activities away from the home and had not spent much time with her daughter.

When the mother called, she had hoped for a simple solution which would solve the "car problem." But there was no simple solution because the situation was a family predicament, not a car problem. And emerging from this predicament called for not just limiting and structuring the daughter's activities more carefully, but also (and this would be much more difficult) getting reacquainted with her daughter and rebuilding a relationship of trust.

## Understanding and Controlling Separation Anger

Parents who succumb to anxiety and grasp their children too tightly will usually make them so uncomfortable that the family will have to deal with the second emotion that goes with separation—anger. And anger, like anxiety, is very contagious. If teenagers become angry, parents often react angrily. Now even at this stage a predicament can be avoided if the involved persons work at conflict resolution and talk about the real issues. However, if they avoid talking about what really separates them, they will probably "say things they don't mean."

The family predicament then moves to a revenge situation. When people "say things they don't mean," actually they are usually referring to things they've said which *were meant* to hurt the other person. We rarely say things we don't mean to say. We say things which may get us into trouble but we usually *mean* to say them.

Dean and Marilyn had two girls in their middle teens. Dean worked on a night shift in a factory, usually six days a week. He saw the girls only briefly in the mornings and on weekends, and did not have much more time than that with his wife. The girls were seeking more freedom, with the most abrasive issue being the time they should be home from dates. The parents worked in advance at establishing times the girls should get home. However, sometimes a special situation would occur requiring a decision on a specific evening. Dean was almost never there so the decision-making role fell to Marilyn alone. At these times she felt lonely and "ganged-up-on" by the girls, who gave many reasons for staying out a little later that particular night. She resented the girls for their "selfishness" and Dean for his absence. The girls resented both parents, but particularly their father. When he tried to intervene, the girls were quite disrespectful and told him he was gone so much he didn't really know what was going on (which was true) with the strong implication that he didn't care (which was not true). So the family plunged deeper and deeper into their predicament of anger and revenge. During this time they were attending all the meetings of their church, although the girls were going under protest because they didn't have any friends their own age in the church.

It became clear that the girls wanted to see more of their father. Even though he did love them, they had little evidence of this because of his lack of time investment with them. When Dean became aware of their need, he found the energy to take a radical approach to the predicament—he changed his life style. Over a period of time he was able to find another job. It paid less, but it was a daytime job which permitted him to be home evenings. He got reacquainted with the girls, and the power struggle began to diminish. Marilyn appreciated seeing more of Dean and found that with her needs for love being met, she was gaining strength to intervene more effectively with the girls. Dean's step which made the changes possible was a radical one because it got at the roots of the predicament, in the same way radical surgery gets at the roots of cancer. Life style requires a great deal of determination to change.

## Pascal's Advice on Intervening without Arousing Anger

I don't like to shop—except in second-hand stores. When I was in graduate school, we bought nearly all of our clothes at second-hand stores. I still buy an occasional pair of used tennis shoes for $1.00 or make some other "find." My most cherished find was the multi-volume set of *The Harvard Classics*, which I bought for 25¢ a volume at a Goodwill store. Volume 48 of this set is the *Thoughts and Minor Works of Pascal*. Blaise Pascal had a brief, stormy life which lasted from 1623 to 1662. A Christian, he is remembered chiefly for his mathematical contributions and for his depth of insight into human nature.

As I read through this dusty old volume I came to appreciate Pascal's ideas about talking with those who differ from us on a particular issue. This bachelor from a different age has much to say to modern families. There is one particular bit of advice he gave that I have worked hard to incorporate into the way I talk with others.

> When we wish to correct with advantage, and to show another that he errs, we must notice from what side he views the matter, for on that side it is usually true, and admit that truth to him, but reveal to him the side on which it is false. He is satisfied with that, for he sees that he was not mistaken, and that he only failed to see all sides. Now, no one is offended at not seeing everything; but one does not like to be mistaken, and that perhaps arises from the fact that man naturally cannot see everything, and that naturally

he cannot err in the side he looks at, since the perceptions of our senses are always true.[5]

Pascal's advice has many implications for parents. First, it requires us to listen very carefully to what our children are saying to us in order to find out exactly how they view a situation. Then it requires that we express our agreement with the truth of their perception. Only then do we reveal an additional side which they may not have seen. This method will avoid many needless power struggles and will often maintain and increase an involvement between parents and children.

The two conversations which follow are given as examples of the power struggle approach (Conversation A) and the Pascal approach (Conversation B). Both conversations are between a mother (M) and her seventeen-year-old daughter (D).

CONVERSATION A

M. I notice you've been spending a lot of time with Julie lately.
D. Sure, she's my friend.
M. What's wrong with your other friends?
D. What's wrong with Julie?
M. Well, Cindy, she has different standards of right and wrong than we do.
D. So ... I don't understand.
M. I just don't want her to influence you to do some of the things she does.
D. You don't trust me! Mom, you can't choose my friends for me.
M. I'm not trying to choose your friends for you, I'm—
D. Yes, you are. I like Julie, and I want to spend time with her (Cindy raises her voice).
M. I'm trying to help you but you won't listen.
(The conversation stops at this point.)

## 189 : IT'S HARD TO LET GO!

CONVERSATION B
M. I notice you've been spending a lot of time with Julie lately.
D. Sure, she's my friend.
M. What do you like most about her?
D. Oh, I don't know. It's just fun being with her.
M. Sounds like you enjoy her care-free attitude.
D. Yes, she doesn't seem to worry about anything, and she really enjoys life and I like that.
M. I can understand why you like being with someone who's so easy-going. An additional way to look at it is that your method of thinking things through carefully before you make a decision has a lot going for it, too.
D. You mean Julie's impulsive?
M. What do you think?
D. I think ... well, sometimes she is. What are you trying to tell me?
M. That even though you respect and admire Julie, I want to encourage you to trust your own way of making a decision about what's right and what's wrong. It's OK to think something through. What do you think about looking at it this way?
D. Well ... sure, I buy that (The conversation continues).

In Conversation A, anger has surfaced because of the power struggle, and the involvement between mother and daughter is disrupted. Both persons are hard at work defending their own point of view with such vigor that they are failing to appreciate the other's point of view.

In Conversation B, the mother listens carefully so she can find the truth in her daughter's perception. She resonates (echoes, agrees) with that truth, and *then* offers an additional point of view. This maintains and strengthens the involvement between the two.

Pascal's method may be seen by some as lacking strength because it purposely seeks to avoid a power struggle. Actually it is a powerful conversational approach because it requires keen listening and a *respect* for the other person. This element of respect is a key to maintaining involvement with our children while at the same time we are letting them go.

## Questions
1. Are you satisfied with the extent to which you have "let go" of your children?
2. Does your life style allow you enough time to really get to know your children?
3. Will you this week put to use with your children Pascal's advice on conversing? Remember, if this is a new way of talking for you, it will seem uncomfortable but that doesn't mean it's phony—just that it's new.
4. In what ways do you let your children know you respect them?

# CHAPTER SEVENTEEN: IT HELPS TO GET CLOSE IF YOU WANT TO GET AWAY

If you are a teenager, this chapter is for you. If you are an adult and you do not yet have the relationship you want with your parents, this chapter is for you also.

## Developmental Tasks

One of the key concepts in psychology is that of developmental tasks.[1] A developmental task is a skill that one develops, or an achievement that one makes at a given time in life, such as walking, talking, doing arithmetic, or preparing for a job. Success in that task leads to a better developed personality and success at later developmental tasks. Failure at that task causes problems in personality development and may cause failure in later developmental tasks. For example, one developmental task is learning to read. Most people spend from kindergarten to about Grade 3 learning to read. Then they make the transition from *learning to read* to *reading to learn* at about the fourth grade level. Failure to make this transition causes problems in later developmental tasks. If one still has not learned to read well by the time he is sixteen, he may fail at another developmental task—learning to drive, because he cannot successfully complete the written part of the driver's test. So the developmental tasks are all woven together.

The most important developmental task that a teenager has to achieve—gaining independence—rests upon success in many other earlier developmental tasks, such as learning to relate to parents, accepting responsibilities for one's actions, and developing a well-thought-out set of values. The struggle for independence, and it is a struggle, is not just to wrestle the right to become independent from one's parents, but it is also to earn that right by becoming a fully functioning man or woman. The barriers to independence are most often inside one's self.

Al and Vicki, an eighteen-year-old couple, loved each other but their love was being scarred over by the hurt and anger they were feeling towards one another. They agreed Al's relationship to his parents was the focus of most of their arguments. Vicki said Al was too dependent on his mother and father. He had not separated himself either geographically (they lived a block from his parent's home) or psychologically from them when he got married. Al saw the situation differently. "Sure, we go over to the folks fairly often. They like us to. Vicki thinks they don't accept her, but they do."

# 193 : GET CLOSE IF YOU WANT TO GET AWAY

Vicki replied that she was jealous because Al sat closer to his mother than he did to her, and in other ways she felt as if she were transparent—that nobody recognized her presence.

The evidences began to be compelling that Al was very much dependent on his mother. Vicki had been unable to help him deal with his dependence because she expressed her anger at him rather than expressing her hurt feelings. This made Al defensive and angry, and then he needed to be with his parents again just to feel good about himself once more. They both sincerely wanted to change the situation but they didn't know how.

The person who is in the middle of the struggle for independence wants to be separated from his parents. Yet, separation from one's loved ones nearly always carries with it some anxiety. Separation anxiety is one reason little children don't want to go to bed. They are anxious about being separated from their parents. The separation anxiety hits us again as teenagers when we think about moving out and being on our own.

## A Paradox

The teenager must get close to his parents in order to push away and become independent. If the apron strings are stretched too tightly due to tension, it is hard to untie them. There are more hands there to undo the knot if the involved persons are close. The string can be cut at either end, and sometimes this is necessary, but often the *emotional* tie is severed and the *dependent* connection remains. To use a Western illustration, you can't unhitch a horse from a wagon if the horse is kicking.

A dependent person is one who hasn't developed the ability to face life without relying on, or blaming another person or other persons. Some people run away because that is the only way they can see they can become independent. But just being separated geographically from one's parents does not bring about independence. The adolescent living a thousand miles from his parents is still dependent on them if he is *reacting* to them; if his life style is based on a reaction pattern, instead of being freely chosen, he is dependent. The term "runaway" itself indicates dependence. If he were independent, he would walk away.

## Rehearsing Doesn't Work

Many people are not aware when they need to talk to another family member about their relationship, or about any conflict that needs to be resolved. The best single sign of needing to talk I have observed in myself is when I find myself *rehearsing* in my own mind what I want to say to the other person and thinking what that person will reply to me. If you think, I really need to tell my dad "I wish you would trust me more," and in your mind you can hear him replying, "What do you mean, I don't trust you?" or "I'll trust you more when you earn it," then this is the clue that you need to get the conversation out of your head into real life.

One reason the rehearsing (dry run) method is used is that we are afraid the other person is not going to listen to us. Therefore, we try to figure out what he is going to say so we can frame a more effective reply. Thus we rehearse a competitive interchange of remarks. This sets up a win-lose situation when we actually do get together. At that time we want to win—to persuade—so we work much harder at *being understood* than at *understanding*.

Jesus taught that if we are to come before a group and give an answer for our faith, we should not think ahead of time what we are going to say, but realize that the Lord will tell us what to say when the time comes. Now, obviously this is not a family situation. But could it be that whenever we are facing a difficult interpersonal situation, we do ourselves a disservice by rehearsing ahead of time, because we never know what the other person will reply? This means that if we rehearse ahead of time, then we are essentially giving a *speech*, instead of really having a *dialogue* with the other person, which requires intense listening.

## Express Appreciation

In talking with your parents it is helpful to remember the three guidelines that were given earlier about communication—it should be warm, straight, and strong. Let's suppose you are a twenty-year-old college student who comes home during the summer to work. On the morning after those nights when you are out on a date, your mother always asks you about where you were the night before and what you did. You find yourself resenting this, but not knowing how to change the situation. One approach that has worked well for some youth is the use of the word "appreciate." It works like this. After your mother has said to you, "Where did you go with Jean last night?" your reply could go this way, "I appreciate your caring for me and I understand this is why you ask the questions you do. But when you quiz me every morning about what I did the night before, it makes me feel like a little boy again and as if you don't trust me. Let's make a deal. If you don't ask me so many questions, I'll begin to share with you more of the things that are happening in my life." Communication like this is not often used and that's the reason many parent-youth conversations are win-lose struggles. You can by-pass the win-lose situation if you begin with the word "appreciate," then tell your parent how you would like them to change, and how you will change.

You may be thinking, "This conversation bit I just read looks artificial to me." If it makes you uncomfortable to read it, this means you have not yet learned to talk this way. It will seem unnatural for you to begin. But the fact that something seems uncomfortable doesn't mean it lacks genuineness. It will seem wooden at first, but as you continue to use it, you'll find this tender-tough way to communicate will become more natural, and that it works.

## Reconciliation

If you and your parents have become angry at each other and this anger has turned into bitterness, then reconciliation will be necessary. The theme of reconciliation between youth and their parents is a powerful one. Such a reconciliation occurs with the young man who is the main character in the Billy Graham film *Time to Run*. It occurs also in *Love Story*.[2] In *Love Story*, Oliver hates his father and is dependent on him. At the end of the story he becomes independent when, in his grief over Jenny's death, he embraces his father. In a sense, Jenny's death has acted as a sacrifice that made reconciliation possible.

It is one of the foremost themes of the Christian faith that reconciliation is not possible without sacrifice. This is dramatically illustrated in the cross, which is at the center of the Christian faith. Human beings were in rebellion against God. Jesus sacrificed his life to bring about reconciliation. As a result persons who have accepted this reconciliation have found new freedom.

To begin the reconciliation process, the dependent person

and his parents must begin talking about the predicaments they know exist but have chosen not to discuss, and they must begin to express their caring for each other in a straight way. Also (and this is the stinger) it is better for the adolescent to initiate the encounter because parents are ordinarily less aware of the dependent relationship, and psychologically they are not in a good position to take the initiative. If they make the first move, once again they are playing the dominant role. It is up to the younger person to take the initiative. One of the marks of maturity is that the youth begins to work on conflict resolution with those close to him.

As I said earlier, the suggestions given here are not only for youth but are for adults at any age whose parents are still living and where there is some estrangement or psychological distance between them. A common myth is that if you don't make it with your parents by the time you are eighteen, you might as well give up. Actually, many very close relationships are firmly established after the "child" is in his twenties or thirties or forties, or even at a later time.

Maxine, a woman in her early fifties, said she felt like a child whenever she was with her mother. Because her mother lived with her for a few months each year, Maxine's burden was a heavy one. Her mother would tell her what to do and Maxine, though she resented it, usually followed the directions even if she knew the results would not be right. Then Maxine learned to use the word "appreciate," and to talk with her mother in a warm, straight, strong way. The showdown came one evening when Maxine was preparing dinner for company. Her mother told her how to prepare the steaks, saying that she realized that Maxine never had done this just right. Maxine replied, "Mother, I appreciate your wanting me to become your perfect girl. But I'm not perfect and I'm not a girl. I'd like to ask you not to treat me like a girl any more by telling me how to do my work." Maxine said later that this was a beginning of a new relationship between the two of them. Her mother began to see her as an adult and to talk with her like one. As a result Maxine is no longer dependent on her mother and they are enjoying a much closer relationship.

## A Way to Look at Your Parents

When was the first time you saw your parent as a person with a life of his or her own? Do you see them this way now? One of the main things you want from your parents is that they not wear you like a badge, that they not see you as an extension of themselves, but that they see you as an individual person in your own right. Now often it is not possible for this to happen until you have come to the place, if you have not already done this, where *you* view your parents in a similar way—not just as your parents, but persons with their own lives, their own goals, their own dreams.

Try a fantasy in which you look out at the world through the eyes of each of your parents. Start with your mother; imagine you are a woman her age, with her husband and her children, her background, her temperament, her health, her voice, her appearance, her needs, her money, her future (as you think it will be), her friends, her relationship to God, and her meaning in life. Then talk to her about this experience. Do the same with your father. You will find yourself separating from your parents in one way as you do this, but drawing closer to them in another way. And that's what becoming independent from your parents is all about.

## You Are a Model

An honest, somewhat shy man in his thirties sat in my office this week talking about his family. He spoke of the future and said that when he got old, it would mean a great deal to him to have his three children visit him. He expected to have a close relationship with them, and that they would want to see him. Yet, when he discussed his relationship with his own parents, he acknowledged that he rarely went to see them because the relationship was an "uncomfortable" one. I asked him why he thought his children would react differently than he did as they grew older.

Parents are models for their children—even in parent-child relationships. Your children will observe you carefully to see how close you are to your parents. If they see you involved in a loving relationship with your parents, and spending time with them when possible, the chances are they will follow your pattern. What you are doing today, in terms of achieving closeness with your parents, may have long-lasting results.

## Questions

1. Do you have the kind of relationship you want with your parents? If not, are you willing to take the initiative in changing it?

# SIX: BEYOND PREDICAMENTS

We can live richer lives with fewer predicaments by:

1. Working to understand each family member's unique learning style, and unique method of expression; and by
2. Spending less "head time" thinking and worrying about how each family member is going to "turn out."

## CHAPTER EIGHTEEN: YOU MEAN A PARENT HAS TO BE A TEACHER, TOO?

Scripture says teaching is an important activity. The word "teach" (and its other forms, such as "taught" and "teaching") is used 239 times in the Bible.[1] This does not count synonyms, e.g., "instruct," which are used many additional times. In both the Old Testament and New Testament, parents are commanded to teach their children.

> And these words which I command you this day shall be upon your heart; and you shall teach them diligently to your children, and shall talk of them when you sit in your house, and when you walk by the way, and when you lie down, and when you

rise. And you shall bind them as a sign upon your hand, and they shall be as frontlets between your eyes. And you shall write them on the doorposts of your house and on your gates (Deuteronomy 6:6-9).

Fathers, do not provoke your children to anger, but bring them up in the discipline (teaching) and instruction of the Lord (Ephesians 6:4).

So, the Bible is unmistakably clear on the answer to the question posed by the chapter title; yes, parents have to be teachers, too. As Christians parents who take our teaching responsibility seriously, we are obligated to find out *how* our children learn. If we know the following two truths about the learning process, we know a great deal about how to teach: 1) All children learn in the same way; and 2) Every child learns in a different way. Just because these two ideas look contradictory, don't throw them out yet. Let's look at each one separately.

## All Children Learn in the Same Way

The evidences from research, our own observations, and common sense show several principles which apply to all learners. Some of these principles, along with a way or two that Christian parents can apply them, are listed below.

1. PRINCIPLE: WE LEARN BY IMITATION. From infancy through adulthood, we can often be observed copying others' actions and characteristics. For example, in one high school I taught in, there was a very skilled football coach who had an unusual mannerism. When the going got tough in a game, he would put a chew of tobacco in his mouth and walk up and down the sidelines with his hands clasped behind his back, chewing vigorously, and sometimes spitting. During one game, when we were one touchdown behind, I happened to observe the coach, who had moved into his stress

ritual. In a procession behind him, much like a duck and ducklings, marched four ninth-graders with similar body positions. They also were chewing tobacco and occasionally spitting, despite a rather sickly look on some of their faces. They admired the coach, and they were imitating one of his behaviors. This action had nothing to do with his success as a coach, but it was one which they could copy.

Imitation plays a powerful role in our lives, especially in the lives of youth. One of my tasks is to train teachers, and I've found that teachers usually teach as they are taught, not as they are taught to teach. Therefore, when a student teacher says to me, "I'll never be like that teacher I used to have," I reply, "The chances are you will become just like him unless you work very hard to find a better way."

Another example of learning by imitation is parents, who usually relate to their children the way they observed their own parents relating to them. If a boy grows up being abused by his parents, the chances are greater he will become a child-abuser. If a girl grows up with parents who touch and hug her, she will likely hug her own children. If she grows up in a home where there is little touch, she will also probably establish an "antiseptic," nontouching environment.

APPLICATION: DO THOSE THINGS YOU WOULD LIKE YOUR CHILDREN TO DO AND DON'T DO THOSE THINGS YOU WISH THEM NOT TO DO. For example, a boy is more likely to value reading if he sees his father reading. If his father *says* reading is important but doesn't read much, the boy gets the message. If the parents are absolutely honest in their social and business relationships, their children are likely to be honest. Everyone is aware of this particular learning principle of imitation, but it is remarkable how often we act as if what we say is more important than what we do. Therefore, this learning principle and the others that follow are not given as new information, but rather as reminders.

2. PRINCIPLE: PERSONS LEARN BETTER WHEN THEY *ASK* TO BE TAUGHT SOMETHING. The first universities in the middle ages were started by students who got together, hired a teacher, and asked him to teach them whatever it was they wanted to learn. Present-day colleges and universities hire teachers who get students together and ask them to learn whatever it is they want to teach. This makes the teaching process considerably more difficult. But it is still possible for the teacher and for the parent to teach if they can get the learner to ask a question. In fact, the student, or child, probably does not become a learner until he does ask a question. How then can we get our children to ask questions?

APPLICATION: STIMULATE CHILDREN TO ASK QUESTIONS. THEN TAKE TIME TO ANSWER THEM. When God brought the people of Israel through the overflowing Jordan with dry feet, he told them to take twelve stones from the river and set them up in Gilgal so that "when your children ask their fathers in time to come, 'What do these stones mean?' then you shall let your children know, 'Israel passed over this Jordan on dry ground' " (Joshua 4:21b, 22). This was to be done so they would know that "the hand of the Lord is mighty."

We have some objects and activities that still cause children to ask questions. When children ask about the symbol of the cross, or about the bread and the cup in communion, or about baptism, we should be prepared with accurate, interesting answers. Is it possible that our children ask us many questions, e.g., "Where did I come from?" and "Why do people have to work?" that we could use to teach them about God's creation and plan for his children? The plain truth is that many parents do not welcome questions from their children, or at least do not give them a high priority. So we get

## 207 : A PARENT HAS TO BE A TEACHER, TOO?

down to a question for ourselves—How much time and energy am I willing to invest in stimulating my children to ask questions, and in answering their questions?

3. PRINCIPLE: CHILDREN LEARN BETTER WHEN THE LEARNING ACTIVITY IS ENJOYABLE. Education has not generally been recognized as being much fun. Many youth have already formed a philosophy of education: Teaching is punitive and learning is painful ("That'll teach you a lesson!"). However, Einstein, one of the most learned persons of this century, had the point of view that joy is the chief motivating factor in all learning, "The most important motive for work in the school and in life is the pleasure in work, pleasure in its result, and the knowledge of the value of the result to the community."[2]

APPLICATION: WHENEVER POSSIBLE, MAKE LEARNING FUN. The producers of Sesame Street have used the application of this principle very effectively. Parents can learn a great deal about how to make learning fun by watching similar television shows which are educational in nature. Puppets can be used. Bible stories can be role-played as well as told. Those who have gone to summer camps know that a peak learning (and fun) experience is the acting out of some event described in the Bible.

That children have fun *expressing* themselves in a role play provides an important clue about learning. Sometimes as parents we act as if our children learn only if we *impress* some truth on them. Another way to look at it is that children (and adults) learn through both impression and expression. Could it be that we underemphasize the importance of learning through expression? Perhaps the only way children can learn to be *creative* is by expression. And such expression is often fun and provides good feelings of accomplishment. A Vacation Bible School teacher told of an incident in which she observed this joy in creating. During crafts her group was learning how to make plaster of Paris plaques with the Christian symbol of the fish on them. Near the end of the week two boys were looking at their finished product, which seemed a bit rough and somewhat sickly to the adult. But one of the boys, with a big smile on his face and with nearly as much paint on him as on his fish, held it at arm's length and said, "Isn't it beautiful?" Such is the joy of learning to express ourselves.

4. PRINCIPLE: PERSONS LEARN BETTER WHEN THEY ARE REWARDED IMMEDIATELY FOR THEIR ACCURATE LEARNING. This principle of immediate positive reinforcement is among the best researched of all learning principles. In our context it means that when a child does a worthwhile act, he is immediately (usually within two or three seconds) given a reward. The reward does not have to be given every time (it is more effective if it is given now and then) and it does not necessarily have to be a material reward such as candy; it can be, for example, a pat on the back.

APPLICATION: OBSERVE YOUR CHILDREN CLOSELY AND OCCASIONALLY GIVE THEM AN IMMEDIATE REWARD FOR A WORTHWHILE ACT. If a child reads a difficult word correctly, makes his bed neatly (or in some cases just makes his bed), does a courteous act for someone, or makes a good moral decision, a "That's good," or a hug or smile increases the chance that the behavior will occur again. Some people see this as manipulation. I see it rather as just being human to another family member. It is perhaps inhuman to be as stingy and tardy as most of us are in giving rewards to our children.

5. PRINCIPLE: PEOPLE LEARN MORE EFFECTIVELY IF THE LEARNING HAS MEANING TO THEM RIGHT NOW. It usually doesn't turn children on to tell them they should

learn this because they will need it when they grow up and they "will be glad then" they did it. Adults can work fairly well with delayed goals, but children do not accept them very well.

APPLICATION: TEACH CHILDREN SOMETHING THAT MAKES SENSE TO THEM OR HELPS THEM RIGHT AT THE MOMENT. You can help your child write a thank-you card to a friend who gave him a present for his eighth birthday. This concrete act will help teach him that thankfulness is more an expression of an attitude than just an attitude only. Suppose you are reading Psalm 100 and come to verse 2, "Serve the Lord with gladness, and come before his presence with singing." Instead of trying to teach your child that it is a good thing to be glad, it might be more effective to ask him what song makes him feel glad, and then sing it with him.

## Every Child Learns in a Different Way

"Instructors here don't know how hard it is for me to learn," said Sharon, "because they don't understand that I don't learn like other students learn. I have a way of learning all my own." Sharon, a college junior, had come for help because she was getting low grades in her classes despite her hard work. She said it had been this way all the way through elementary school and junior and senior high school, as well as college. But she had just begun to hear about learning disabilities (a condition in which persons are lacking not in intelligence but in the ability to get information in and out effectively) and she wondered if there was something that might be done to help her.

She took a series of tests through which she discovered,

among other things, that she was bright—in the upper one-fourth of the population in intelligence. But this only raised another question—"OK, if I'm smart, why can't I learn?"

The evidence was becoming clear by this time that she could learn, but that she had to learn in her own unique learning style. She remembered accurately material that was given in a lecture. On the other hand, she read slowly and she did not remember correctly what she had read. Her strong input channel, then, seemed to be hearing and her weak input channel, reading. In terms of output she was a poised, able speaker but she had a great deal of difficulty writing information that was clear and coherent. Overall, then, her *strong* learning channel was auditory-vocal (hearing-saying) and her *weak* learning channel was visual-motor (reading-writing).

There were other examples of her unique learning style. She could not readily pull a letter of the alphabet, such as "e," from her mind. She needed to sequence the alphabet up to that point in order to "retrieve" that letter. In other words, in her mind she would say "a b c d e." She did the same thing with numbers. Her laterality was undeveloped, that is, she did not automatically know left from right. She had to use a ring on her finger or some other clue in order to figure which was which.

She discussed how difficult mathematics had always been for her. I asked her to add 8 and 5. She paused a moment before she gave the answer, and during this pause she tapped her pencil on the table five times. What she had done was to use her strong auditory sense to go from 8 to 13 by adding to the number 8 the taps she sounded on the table. None of her arithmetic functions were automatic. Throughout her life, Sharon had had to work much harder than the average learner, even though she herself was above average in intellectual skills, just in order to make it in school.

So other college students volunteered to help Sharon. Three of them acted as readers for her. They read dramas to her, history books, and other reading assignments. This required scores of hours of Sharon's time and of the volunteer readers' time. She took the initiative of seeing each one of her instructors and explaining to them how she learned and what her strong and weak learning channels were. Some of them arranged oral tests for her. Others gave her longer periods of time to write her tests. As a result the following semester she earned all A's and B's in her courses. This kind of change would not have been possible with everyone. She had a strong quest for learning that made her willing to work very hard to find new ways to learn. Her experience illustrates the saying, "If persons don't learn the way we teach them, we'd better teach them the way they can learn."

Sharon had a learning disability. This is not true of most learners. On the other hand, what *is* true of most learners is that one learning style usually works better for them than others. Each person has a learning style as unique as his fingerprint. And this is what is meant by the statement, "Every child learns in a different way."

## The Different Learning Channels

There are many aspects of learning styles. We will look at one—channels of learning—probably the most useful and perhaps the most overlooked component of learning styles. We use learning channels to get information in and out.

There are a number of learning channels but we will work with only the three most important channels. Any input that comes in through the eyes is visual. Any output going through the hands is described as motor. The best example of this, as mentioned with Sharon above, is reading and writing. Schools have usually been operated as if all children were strong in the visual-motor channel. Only in the last ten years, with the discovery of new information in the learning disabilities area, has it been found that schools can no longer assume that all children can learn to read in the first few grades and then read to learn the rest of their time in school. Sharon is an example of a person who is stronger in the auditory-vocal channel than the visual-motor channel. This person effectively stores, understands, and retrieves information which comes in through the ears.

A third learning channel is haptic-motor. Haptic refers to learning through touch or through movement. For example, a child who has a weak visual-motor channel may be taught to recognize letters of the alphabet by making them with clay or by feeling sandpaper letters. He learns through his fingertips. Some children find it helpful to say a word with their lips when they are reading it. Using the lips while reading used to be discouraged because it was considered inefficient. It is now commonly recognized by educators that there are some children who need this crutch for awhile because they cannot get a good enough "grip" on a word by seeing it; they have to *feel* the different position of the mouth muscles as they say the word silently.

One way to understand the concept of learning channels is to imagine that you live in a TV viewing area where you are able to get three channels, only one of which gives you good reception. A second channel is fair, although the fidelity may be poor and it may have some "snow." Let's suppose that the third channel is very weak. You have to work hard just to get the main idea of a given program on that channel. This is somewhat like learning channels, because often one may be strong and another weak.

## 213 : A PARENT HAS TO BE A TEACHER, TOO?

You may be asking the question, "So people have three main learning channels. What does this have to do with my relationship with my children?" The value of understanding strong and weak learning channels is that if we can discover our children's strong learning channels, then we are in a better position to teach them. One parent said to me, for example, that the main problem in his relationship with his twelve-year-old son was that his son was disobedient. I asked him to specify exactly what he meant. He replied that his boy didn't do what he told him to do. He was a farmer and he often told his boy three or four things to do at chore time. Sometimes his boy would do two of these and let the others go or sometimes he would do all four in reverse order. It was discovered through diagnostic testing that this boy had poor auditory sequential memory. It was not that he chose to "forget" the instructions his father gave him. It was that he simply could not store and retrieve these oral instructions in the correct sequence. When his father learned to use a visual channel and write the chores to be done on the bulletin board, the boy was usually able to carry out his assignments satisfactorily.

Another auditory problem that sometimes shows up is a figure-ground deficiency. Some people don't like to do small group work. In some instances these persons have an auditory figure-ground problem, that is, they are unable to focus on the person in the group who is talking. They hear many sounds around the room. Often they hear a participant in another group more clearly than one in their own group. They do not differentiate well enough between the person they need to be listening to (figure) from background noises (ground). It is helpful to observe our family members to see if they pick up readily on what it is they need to be listening to. (Incidentally, this does not mean that they have to sit very still.

Often the person who is moving the most is listening the best.)

Another example of how important it is to know children's strong and weak learning channels can be seen with the child who is caught stealing in school, or shoplifting downtown. The typical school official or parent will "lecture" the child regarding the evils of stealing. This is usually ineffective, for several reasons. One important reason is that the person who shoplifts is usually a *visual* person. They see something, they want it, and sometimes they take it. The adult who is an impulsive buyer and cannot trust himself or herself with a credit card is another example of a visual person. With these persons generally the auditory channel is their weak channel. Therefore a lecture usually does not find its mark. A much more effective consequence of shoplifting is that the shoplifter would be shown a flip chart similar to an insurance salesman's flip chart in which there are pictures or drawings of the child who takes something that does not belong to him, and then there are successive pictures of that child being confronted by a store manager, a policeman, parents, juvenile authorities, a judge, and other persons he might reasonably be expected to see. This is a powerful influence and a stronger deterrent to a visual learner.

There are several advantages of knowing the strong and weak learning channels of our children. If we know our child's strong learning channel we know much better how to help him with homework. If we are helping a child review for a test and the child is a visual learner, it may help to write out sample questions for him. If he is an auditory learner, it may be more effective to *ask* him the questions. In terms of getting things done around the house, it is helpful to know which of our children learn in which ways. We may choose to use the bulletin boards for the visual learners and oral directions for the auditory-vocal learning child.

## Bibliotherapy

If we have a middle child who is feeling pressed from both directions, and we want to help him so that he does not feel so much alone, we need first to discover his strong learning channel. If he is an auditory learner, our primary method of intervening may be to talk with him. If he is a strong visual-motor learner, we may best direct him to books, such as the *The Middle Moffat*,[3] or *Molly in the Middle*.[4] This bibliotherapy approach (working with personality and emotional development through suggesting selected books) is being used more and more by teachers, and offers to parents a seldom-used but powerful tool in working with their children.

If you are interested in the area of bibliotherapy, and want to learn more of the guidelines for its use, and find further books to recommend to your children, you may find the following books and articles helpful:

*Bibliotherapy and Its Widening Applications*, by Eleanor Frances Brown (Matuchen, New Jersey: Scarecrow Press, Inc., 1975).

*Bibliotherapy: Methods and Materials*, by the Committee on Bibliotherapy, Mildred T. Moody, Chairman, and the Sub-Committee on the Troubled Child, Hilda K. Limper, Chairman, (Chicago: Association of Hospital and Institution Libraries, American Library Association, 1971).

"Children's Literature Can Affect Coping Behavior," *Personnel and Guidance Journal*, 43:897-903, 1965.

*Facilitating Human Development Through Reading: The Use of Bibliotherapy in Teaching and Counseling*, by Joseph S. Zaccaria and Harold A. Moses (Champaign, Ill.: Stipes, 1968).

If you want to read some or all of these books, the least expensive method is to check them out from your local library.

If your library does not have them, they can usually get them for you through interlibrary loan. In this way you can see if they would be valuable enough to you to purchase. Most of these books have extensive bibliographies which will provide you with many other possible resources.

## A Way to Discover the Strong Learning Channel

We have looked at some of the advantages of knowing which learning channels are strongest in our children. We've also seen some ways of working through the strong channel. Once you decide such an approach is valuable, the next step is discovering the strong channel.

How can you find the strong learning channel of your child? The "Checklist for Discovering Learning Channels" should prove helpful to you for this purpose. It provides sixteen items in each of the three channels. Most of the items are useful in studying the learning channels of a child, adolescent, or adult.

The checklist will help you discover the unique learning style of your children. Make a check mark by the items under the three headings that describe most accurately the way your child functions in a given activity. For example, if he can put a model together correctly using written instructions, this is one evidence that he is a visual learner. If on the other hand he prefers to work with another person who reads the instructions to him, this would indicate that he may be an auditory learner. If he chooses to feel the different parts and put them together without referring to instructions, this may indicate that he is a haptic learner. No single item is enough to enable one to draw conclusions about the learning style of another person. However, if you find most of your

# CHECKLIST FOR DISCOVERING LEARNING CHANNELS

### I. STRONG IN VISUAL CHANNEL

___ 1. Likes to keep written records
___ 2. Typically reads billboards while driving or riding
___ 3. Puts model together correctly using written directions
___ 4. Follows written recipes easily when cooking
___ 5. Reviews for a test by writing a summary
___ 6. Expresses self best by writing
___ 7. Writes on napkins in a restaurant
___ 8. Can put a bicycle together from a mail order house using only the written directions provided
___ 9. Commits a Zip Code to memory by writing it
___ 10. Uses visual images to remember names
___ 11. A "bookworm"
___ 12. Writes a note to compliment a friend
___ 13. Plans the upcoming week by making a list
___ 14. Prefers written directions from employer
___ 15. Prefers to get a map and find own way in a strange city
___ 16. Prefers reading-writing games like "Scrabble"

### II. STRONG IN AUDITORY CHANNEL

___ 1. Prefers to have someone else read instructions when putting a model together
___ 2. Reviews for a test by reading notes aloud or by talking with others
___ 3. Expresses self best by talking
___ 4. Talks aloud when working a math problem
___ 5. Prefers listening to a cassette over reading the same material
___ 6. Commits Zip Code to memory by saying it
___ 7. Uses rhyming words to remember names
___ 8. Calls on the telephone to compliment a friend
___ 9. Plans the upcoming week by talking it through with someone
___ 10. Talks to self
___ 11. Prefers oral directions from employer
___ 12. Likes to stop at a service station for directions in a strange city
___ 13. Prefers talking-listening games
___ 14. Keeps up on news by listening to the radio
___ 15. Able to concentrate deeply on what another person is saying
___ 16. Uses "free" time for talking with others

### III. STRONG IN TOUCH-MOVEMENT CHANNEL

___ 1. Likes to build things
___ 2. Uses sense of touch to put a model together
___ 3. Can distinguish items by touch when blindfolded
___ 4. Learns touch system rapidly in typing
___ 5. Gestures are a very important part of communication
___ 6. Moves with music
___ 7. Doodles and draws on any available paper
___ 8. An "out-of-doors" person
___ 9. Likes to express self through painting or dance
___ 10. Moves easily; well-coordinated
___ 11. Spends a large amount of time on crafts and handwork
___ 12. Likes to feel texture of drapes and furniture
___ 13. Prefers movement games to games where one just sits (this may also be a function of age)
___ 14. Finds it fairly easy to "keep fit" physically
___ 15. One of the fastest in a group to learn a new physical skill
___ 16. Uses "free" time for physical activities

(Column with most checks—the strong channel)

marks in one of the columns, then you have some fairly good evidences that your child's strong learning channel is in that area.

Having discovered your child's strong learning area, you will be in an excellent position to provide new information to him/her in any area you choose. An additional guideline is that whenever possible it is helpful if we use *more than one* sensory modality (seeing, hearing, touching). For example, if we want to teach a child to use a power tool, it is helpful to have him read the directions, to talk with him about safety and other procedural matters, and then actually to let him use it under our direction. In this way we use all three channels.

It is significant that God told the Israelite parents to use all three of the sensory modalities in teaching their children. As the passage from Deuteronomy quoted at the beginning of this chapter made clear, the parents were to teach their children by *talking* to them throughout the day as they were involved in different activities. They were also to *write* the great commandment (... You shall love the Lord your God with all your heart, and with all your soul, and with all your might) on the doorposts of their houses and on the gates. Finally, the Lord instructed the Israelite parents to use three-dimensional objects, such as the stack of twelve stones, so the children might *touch* as well as see this reminder of the greatness of God.

## Questions

1. On the line from 1 to 10, shown below, how would you rate yourself as to the *time* you spend teaching your children? With 1 being almost no time invested as a teacher, and 10 being at least an hour a day involved in some teaching-learning activity with them, place a "T" at the appropriate place on the line.

   1   2   3   4   5   6   7   8   9   10

## 219 : A PARENT HAS TO BE A TEACHER, TOO?

2. On the line from 1 to 10, shown below, how would you rate yourself as to your *effectiveness* as a teacher of your children? With 1 representing a feeling of failure in your teaching role, and 10 representing an awareness that your children are changing their behavior in a positive way as a result of your teaching, place an "E" at the appropriate place on the line.

1    2    3    4    5    6    7    8    9    10

3. If you are nearer the left end of these lines than you would like to be, let me encourage you to form a plan to change. What will be the first step of your plan?

# CHAPTER NINETEEN: RECEIVING AND SENDING SILENT SIGNALS

Imagine a typical family (There isn't any such thing, so that's why we have to imagine it!) of four sitting at the dinner table. The topic of conversation is interesting and each of the three listeners wants to be the next one to talk. They try to reserve the next talking time by giving "nonword" signals. One person moistens her lips with her tongue while leaning forward. Another adjusts his glasses and clears his throat. The third shifts her weight and opens her mouth slightly.

How do *you* reserve talking time when you want to be the next person to talk? Do you know how each member of your family signals for a "reservation"? If not, you may be consistently interrupting others in your family without being aware of it. It is possible to interrupt someone even if they haven't said anything, if they make the first reservation. At this point you may object and say this kind of keen observation is too much to expect. But is it? Have you been offended when you know the others in your family are aware you are the next person to "get the floor," and then someone starts right in without signaling?

We can avoid offending others and escape many family predicaments if we learn to monitor accurately (receive) others' silent signals, and if we increase our ability to express (give) love with our facial expressions and gestures as well as our words.

## Receiving Others' Signals

People not only make bids to talk next, but also communicate other messages, as many as several each second, by body language. Body language is any body movement other than the saying of words. Such language may even involve nonword sounds such as a laugh, yawn, or sigh. Other senses than vision and hearing are involved. For example, a handshake provides touch input. And correctly or incorrectly, people often make judgments about another person on the basis of the nature of the handshake.

We also make judgments about others based on their body position relative to our own. In the musical *The King and I*, the king tells Anna that it is important that her head never be above his. We may take this as an example of a custom of a different age and culture. However, it is interesting to watch children and adults in terms of eye level. Most adults talk to children from "up above." It must be hard on a little child's neck to tip his head back and look up at such a sharp angle. What happens when an adult gets down on eye level with a child? Be prepared for some surprising dialogue if you do this.

A faculty colleague of mine formed the habit years ago of getting on eye level with children whenever he talked to them. He has excellent rapport with children, and can get a dialogue going with children or youth of any age. One day Marv and I visited a local day-care center. Near the door were two children, a boy and a girl, each about three and a half to four years old. Marv knelt down by the bulletin board near which they were standing and asked, "What are you doing?"

"I'm pinning a tail on this tiger (on the bulletin board)," the boy replied. And then, because it was so reinforcing to him to look right straight across to an adult, he carried on the conversation, "Do you ever go tiger hunting!"

"No."

"Why not?"

Marv thought about that one awhile, then said, "I'm afraid of tigers."

"I'm not. I go tiger hunting all the time. When I go tiger hunting, I just bust 'em right in the mouth!"

The little girl had been wanting to get into the conversation because it probably was not often she got to talk to a grownup eye-to-eye either, so she came in with, "When I go tiger hunting, I bite 'em!"

The little boy thought about this awhile and then remarked, "I've found it doesn't work to bite tigers; they just bleed all over you."

It was quite a conversation to behold. The expressive ability of these preschool children was turned loose by a smiling adult who was thoughtful enough to talk with them on their eye level. True, they had a thing or two to learn about separating fantasy from reality—but that could come later. The children had correctly received Marv's body language signal that he wanted to listen to them as well as talk with them.

While it is probably true that nearly everyone "reads" and understands such signals, it also appears true that, as with printed language, some persons are more highly skilled readers than others. For example, people in the helping professions, such as counseling, have to rely heavily on the information gained by observing silent signals. Actually, anyone who wants to understand other family members better can do this by learning to monitor their body language more accurately.

## Two Objections

Some people object to the whole idea of observing body language. One objection is that it is possible to observe others' nonverbal behaviors just to "psych them out." This is a valid objection because nobody wants to be psyched out. On the other hand, the sensitive person monitors others' silent signals, not to psych them out but rather to understand them. And everybody wants to be understood. Your family is saying not only, "Listen to me," but "Look at me," and "Pay attention to me."

Another objection to observing body language goes something like this, "It's absurd to think you can learn something about somebody by just seeing one thing—like the way they cross their legs or move their hands!" I think this is a true statement. But an additional way to look at it is this—the very reason for becoming more skilled in observing such signals is that we learn to "see" many behaviors that we formerly overlooked, and this allows us to make a much more valid conclusion than untrained observational skills permit. Since we usually draw conclusions about others anyway, even if we don't plan to, it is good to have as many evidences available as possible.

## Why Observe Body Language?

Eloise, a woman in her thirties, still remembers going down the hall one day as a high school junior. She had a "secret crush" on a good-looking boy who at that moment was coming up the hall with another boy. She wanted to say something to him but she was so embarrassed and shy that she didn't even *look* at him. Then she heard him say to his friend after they had passed each other, "Boy, is she ever stuck up!" He had totally misunderstood her actions. (On the other hand it needs to be said that she wasn't giving very straight signals.)

Signals are usually more spontaneous than words, and thus often provide more accurate reflections of a person's feelings. Most of our statements are rehearsed, that is, we run a sentence that we are going to say through our minds two or three or more times before we actually say it. Body language, on the other hand, is more often nonrehearsed. A shrug of the shoulders is seldom rehearsed. It may mean, "I don't know," or it may even mean, "I don't know, and I really don't care enough to invest my time and energy in a verbal answer to your question."

Body language almost always is faster communication than words. Listening to a person talk is as if one were reading the printed lines that emerge from a teletype describing traffic at an intersection. Information is provided a word at a time. Observing body language is more like looking from a helicopter at the actual intersection. The information comes, not in a sequence of words, but in an *instantaneous, panoramic* way.

## The Two Steps—
## Observing and Interpreting

It is very important to be able to tell the difference between the signals themselves and their meaning. For example, you may observe your fourteen-year-old boy chewing the eraser of his pencil while he's doing his homework. The statement, "He is chewing his pencil," is a factual observation. The statement, "He is nervous," is an interpretation. He may be nervous or he may not be. There would have to be many other evidences to make this interpretation. There are many reasons for putting things in one's mouth. Observant parents may have noted that oral activity (putting things in one's mouth) increases just before meals when children are hungry and are anticipating eating.

Five statements are made about each of the three persons below. Decide which of the statements describe behaviors and which are interpretations.

1. a. Tony was quite lazy.
   b. Tony was sad.
   c. Tony rested his chin on his left hand.
   d. Tony appeared dejected.
   e. Tony was not very active.
2. a. Jane was happy.
   b. Jane appeared glad.
   c. Jane was hilarious.
   d. Jane was pleasant.
   e. Jane smiled.
3. a. John was cross with his mother.
   b. John got up on the wrong side of the bed.
   c. John stamped his feet.
   d. John was insolent.
   e. John was surly.

To answer the question, "Which of the sentences describe

behaviors?" one needs to decide "Which of the statements name body movements?" Only 1c, 2e, and 3c fit this criterion. It is in distinguishing the difference between *behaviors* and their *interpretations* that the observer sharpens his awareness of another person and increases his ability to help that person.

## A Way to Look at Your Family

As you work at understanding your family through their body language, try to observe each movement. Remember the same body movement may tell you something on one occasion and not on another. For example, a boy may kick a ball without intending to communicate any message. However, if he kicks another boy, he is usually trying to get a message across, such as "I don't like you, and I want to hurt you." Some body language, therefore, is *intended* to communicate a message. Other behaviors may tell you something without the person planning to, such as a facial flush. Still others, such as the blink of an eye, may communicate no message, intended or otherwise.

To provide a better look at body language, you can focus on these four body areas: 1) Head, face, and neck; 2) Arms, hands, and fingers; 3) Trunk; and 4) Legs and feet. It helps to make a conscious effort to be aware of these different areas because many persons focus almost entirely on one area, such as the hands and arms (gestures) or the face (mouth or eye movements).

HEAD, FACE, AND NECK MOVEMENTS
Movements in this area afford a wealth of information for the aware observer. However, in contrast to gestures and other body movements, the movements of the head, face,

and neck are usually small. It requires a high degree of awareness to sense important signals from this area of the body.

Sometimes it takes more than ears to "hear" your children or your spouse cry. A slight moistness of the eyes, a nervous laugh, or a quivering of the voice, when put together with what that person is saying, may tell you that he/she could be crying inside.

Some body language may show conflict. Suppose your husband wants to talk, but is hesitant to risk himself. He may bite his lips, frown, or put his hand to his jaw as if to control his mouth movements. You may help him get it out by saying something like, "It's difficult for you right now to say to me what you need to say." If said in an understanding, not an accusing or interrogating manner, this kind of reflection of feeling is usually helpful.

ARMS, HAND, AND FINGER MOVEMENTS

Movements here are among the most commonly observed actions. It is important to look for the patterns of behaviors or repeated behaviors. A college student, as a part of his assignment in a class, observed a boy. He noticed that the child kept rubbing one of his ears with his fist, so he reported this to the parents. They took him to their family physician who discovered an ear infection. The parents had "seen" the same behavior but they either hadn't *observed* its repetition or they had not attached significance to *(interpreted)* it.

TRUNK MOVEMENTS

Things to look for here include posture. Posture can tell you about physical condition; it can also tell you about mental and emotional outlook. The child who is "down" may be looking down with his eyes and may be stooped slightly in his posture. There are additional clues for one's emotional state. The primary signal that the body gives for discouragement or depression is a deep sigh. Muscle tension in the trunk portion of the body is another emotional indicator.

A woman in her mid-twenties came for counseling. Her posture was somewhat stooped and quite tense. She told of growing up believing that a woman should be submissive and weak. Actually, she had a great deal of personal strength. Therefore, she was constricting herself, holding the strength in and appearing weak. But this pretending was taking its toll in backaches, headaches, and muscle tension. When she gave herself permission to come across the strong woman that she was, her physical symptoms began to disappear. Also, her posture slowly began to improve.

LEG AND FEET MOVEMENTS

Some of the movements here are quite communicative. Have you noticed the different walks of your family members on different days? There is, for example, a bouncy walk, a sprightly walk, a draggy walk, a quiet walk, a slow walk, a determined walk, and a hesitant walk. The way a person is walking can tell you a great deal about how he feels. If you are observing his walk closely, much of the time you will not need to ask a question like "How did school go today?" or "How were things at work?" You can begin in a more understanding way by saying, "Looks like you're enjoying your day," or "It's been a long day." A remark like this lets a person know you care enough to pay attention to him.

## Giving Signals

It is important not only to be aware of the signals our family is giving us, but to be aware of the signals we are *sending* to the rest of our family. Are you sending more positive signals (smiles, friendly eye contact) or negative signals (frowns, angry looks) to your family? This comparison of the number of positive and negative signals we send has been called the Reward-Punishment Ratio (R-P Ratio). The importance of this ratio has been discussed by Robert and Evelyn Kirkhart.[1] They included oral communication as well as body language. So rewards include a "That's fine," a friendly wave, a smile, a pat on the shoulder, or a "Thank you." Punishments include any kind of "putdown" or "discount" such as a scowl, "That's really messy," or "What did you do that for?" The Kirkharts studied over a period of time what effect on children different ratios have. Their findings are striking and of great significance to parents.

> We have observed that a reward to punishment (R-P) ratio of five rewards for every one punishment is about optimal in guiding and directing a child's behavior. However, when the R-P Ratio falls down to only two rewards for every one punishment, neurotic symptoms begin to develop, especially those of inferiority and inadequacy and a generalized fear of the failure. When the R-P Ratio drops further to one-to-one or even below, the child begins to despair of ever winning the adult's approval, and hostile, angry feelings arise. Predelinquent acts are often observed in children who chronically experience this R-P level.[2]

Many parents, instead of having a five-to-one R-P Ratio may have a one-to-one or one-to-five or even lower ratio. I have observed parent-child interactions over a sustained period of time in which the R-P Ratio was probably one-to-twenty, that is, one reward to every twenty punishments. The children and adolescents involved in these situations were extremely discouraged and some of them very hostile. Some were runaways. The Kirkharts tell about one mathematically-oriented father of a severely emotionally disturbed boy who gained insight into his own behavior and decided that his R-P Ratio must be about one-to-five hundred.

A high R-P Ratio does not mean that the child should not be punished. Punishment is sometimes necessary because children need to learn what the limits are. Later, as they internalize their own limits, the need for punishments will diminish.

Although the R-P Ratio includes words as well as body language, we are emphasizing the latter because the effect of that is most often overlooked. Also it is relatively easy to remember a *statement* we make to another family member to see if it is positive or negative. It is more difficult to recall our *body language* to determine its effect.

The reality and effect of nonword communication is shown clearly in the Bible. A great deal of feeling can be communicated through the eyes. In 1 Samuel 18 it is recorded that women sang, "Saul has slain his thousands, and David his ten thousands."

Upon hearing this, Saul became very angry. "And Saul *eyed* David from that day on." When Saul and David's eyes met after this, probably both sensed the jealous death wish that gleamed in Saul's eyes.

There are scores of examples of positive "silent signals" that are recorded in Scripture. When Jacob and Esau met after being apart many years, all their initial communication was without words (Genesis 33). Jacob bowed down seven times. Because of the way he had treated Esau, he wanted to know how Esau felt about him, before they got very close. "But Esau ran to meet him, and embraced him, and fell on his neck and kissed him, and they wept" (vs. 4). Then they began to talk.

## 231 : RECEIVING AND SENDING SILENT SIGNALS

The same sort of scene is pictured in the New Testament, only at a farewell rather than a meeting. After the Apostle Paul had recounted to the elders at Ephesus his ministry to them, he prepared to leave. "And when he had spoken thus, he knelt down and prayed with them all. And they all wept and embraced Paul and kissed him, sorrowing most of all because of the word he had spoken, that they should see his face no more. And they brought him to the ship" (Acts 20:36-38). The kiss, as a greeting, was encouraged by the Apostle. He wrote to the Romans, "Greet one another with a holy kiss. All the churches of Christ greet you" (16:16).

Touching with the hands is perhaps the most often recorded nonword expression in the New Testament. We can learn a great deal about how to give love to our family by examining some of these passages. The laying on of hands was used to transmit power and strength (Acts 6:6 and 13:3). Strength can flow from one person to another through touch.

Touch was also used as a part of the healing process. James asks, "Is any among you sick? Let him call for the elders of the church, and let them pray over him, anointing him with oil in the name of the Lord" (5:14). Touch has nearly always been a part of the getting well process. One of the things a physician does first in the diagnostic process is to palpate (examine by touch) the patient. One of the many striking things about the ministry of our Lord is the frequency with which he used touch. He touched a leper (Matthew 8:3) and cleansed him of his leprosy. He touched the hand of Peter's mother-in-law and healed her of her fever (Matthew 8:15).

Have you noticed that when one person touches others, they feel free to touch back? People often pressed upon Jesus to touch him in order to be healed. But it was not just the ill who wanted to touch him. John often leaned on Jesus as they ate. Mary Magdalene wanted to embrace him after the resurrection, but he told her not to, that he had not yet ascended to the Father (John 20:17). Mary, the sister of Lazarus and Martha, anointed the Lord with ointment and wiped his feet with her hair (John 11:2).

Jesus touched people not only to heal them but also to give them courage. On the Mount of Transfiguration when Moses and Elijah suddenly appeared to talk with Jesus, and when the Father's voice sounded from heaven, Peter, James and John "fell on their faces, and were filled with awe" (Matthew 17:6). Obviously they couldn't see anything with their faces on the ground and their ears may not have been functioning too well after just hearing the very voice of God. What did Jesus do? "But Jesus came and touched them, saying, 'Rise, and have no fear.' And when they lifted up their eyes, they saw no one but Jesus only" (vv. 7, 8).

Your children need your touch to give them courage. They especially need it at bedtime. Sleep means *separation from parents* to little children. And separation nearly always causes anxiety and fear. Reading is fun at bedtime, and one reason for this is that the parent and child are nearly always touching each other as they look at the book. But children need to be touched at other times, too. And older children and youth need touch from their parents. You can get in touch in many ways in addition to the usual ways of hugging and kissing. You can give a back rub or a shoulder rub or a pat on the back.

Does the rest of your family see you as a warm person? Remember that no matter how warm you feel inside, you haven't expressed warmth until the person next to you feels it. Insights are best expressed through words but warmth is best expressed through action. We draw courage from touch, as mentioned above. But for some, and you may be one, it takes courage *to* touch. This courage comes from the Lord, who often touched people's lives by touching their bodies.

## Questions

1. How many times have you touched your children today? This week?
2. How many times have your children touched you today? This week?
3. If you are not satisfied with your answers to the above questions, what is your plan for changing?

# CHAPTER TWENTY: IF THEY JUST TURN OUT ALL RIGHT!

Ruth explained that her predicament as a mother was that her two elementary school-age boys would not mind her. She didn't understand why things were going so badly for her as a mother because she was effective in the other areas of her life. She was one of the leading lay persons in her church. She was able to direct others to get things done. In fact, she was known as a person who, if you had a task that needed to be done, would see that it got done. She managed her home well in terms of efficiency in her tasks. She had a loving relationship with her husband. The thought-provoking question she posed was, "Why is it that

# 235 : IF THEY JUST TURN OUT ALL RIGHT!

I am a success in all other areas but as a mother I'm a zero?"

Many parents, men as well as women, have felt deeply this contrast between their productive lives in terms of work, and what they see as nonproductive lives as parents. Often these parents are extremely active at tasks that have a visible result. They turn out paper work at the office, or machine parts at the factory, complete the many tasks to be done in the home, chair a committee or task force for the church—and feel like a failure as parents.

## Product-Oriented Parents

I finally realized after working with a number of parents who discussed this contrast in their lives that there was a common pattern of behavior in each of their lives. They were all product-oriented people. Whenever there was work to be done, they did it—and felt fulfilled as they viewed the end-product. It needs to be said here that such an attitude has much to be said for it. As someone has observed, "Nothing works, if people don't." On the other hand, these parents were dissatisfied with how their lives were going and desperately wanted to change.

There is one question that is lying deep inside all product-oriented parents—unasked and unanswered. When one asks these parents, "Are you wondering if your children will turn out all right?" the resulting deep sigh reveals that it is a central question in their lives. And it is not inappropriate that this is their foremost question because they see their children as products. Oh, they see them as much more than that, because for the most part they are compassionate people and dedicated Christians who want the very best for their family. But they see through their own grid of producing results and accomplishing tasks, and they cannot feel good about themselves until they are satisfied their main products have turned out all right.

I sometimes carry on a conversation like the following one to show that it is counter-productive to be so product-oriented with our children. (The "C" stands for counselor and the "P" for parent.)

> C. It sounds as if you're really concerned about how your children will turn out.
> P. (With a sigh and nod of the head) Yes.
> C. When will you know when your children have turned out all right? How old will they need to be?
> P. Well—(careful thought) maybe if they're teenagers, fifteen or sixteen or so, and if they've made decisions for Christ and if they're leading worthwhile lives, and—you know—not involved in drugs or anything like that, then I can feel more relaxed and successful.
> C. You can never tell for sure. Sometimes people in their late teens do things you'd never have predicted a few years earlier.
> P. Well, I know that's true. I've seen it happen once in awhile. As a matter of fact, I know I'll feel better when they're in their twenties and are married and starting their families.
> C. I know this doesn't happen very often, but have you noticed that sometimes young people in their twenties adopt a totally different life style than their parents had?
> P. Yes, that's true.
> C. And usually people have settled down by the time they're thirty, but you can't be sure about this. And people in their forties, well I'm sure you've heard of forty-five-year-olds doing some weird things. As a matter of fact, you could be sixty-five or seventy or even older before you'll know for sure how your children have turned out.

About this time the parent begins to see what I'm getting at, that is, that we can *never* know for sure how our children are going to turn out because as long as people are living they are in the process of "turning out."

## Is It O.K. to Play?

Merle had a puzzled expression as he said, "I don't understand it, but I can't seem to play with my kids." His wife and children (a seven-year-old girl and ten-year-old boy) agreed with him. He told about his growing-up days which were filled with hard work, and continued, "It just doesn't seem right for me to be playing with my kids; I'm happiest when I'm working and getting things done. Yet I know I need to spend time with them."

Merle was like other product-oriented parents. He felt best when he was producing. The problem with play was that when it was over there was nothing concrete to show for it. Merle knew that his children liked to play and if he could learn to play with them it would bring about a closer relationship with them; he knew that, but he still had the feeling that playing wasn't quite the right thing for an adult to do. In fact, it was almost as if he were afraid when he sat down to play with his children, his own father would come up, tap him on the shoulder and say, "Back to work."

I have worked with a number of parents like Merle and Ruth who have come to the conclusion they don't know how to play but would like to learn. Nearly all of them have had a dominant, same-sex parent who valued product (getting a task accomplished) but not process (interacting with others, listening, dialoging). I explain to these parents that if they really want to learn how to play, they need to spend time with children because children are the best instructors in a "how-to-play" course.

With some parents, particularly those with school-age children, it has been helpful to get them started with a form of play that does have a product, namely a craft, such as ceramics or modeling. Then after this transition to product-oriented play, some are able to move on to play that is simply process-oriented, that is, play in which there is no product at all, but which is done just for the fun of it. Usually parents who have learned how to *enjoy playing* with their children have children who have learned how to *enjoy working* with their parents.

## Getting Children to Mind

I've noticed in working with families that product-oriented parents usually have more difficulty getting their children under verbal control (a situation where the child does what the parent says without the use of force) than other parents do. This seemed strange to me until two of these parents confided that whenever a "showdown" came, they did not require their children to mind because they were afraid if they did, it would bring about bad feelings and the children would hold this against them and therefore turn out badly. It made sense to me then. Product-oriented parents are so geared to the *future*, they often slide over present predicaments to avoid a touchy situation which could negatively affect the future. Actually, this point of view on the part of the parents caused predicaments. Their children who needed—and lacked—structure, began to manipulate the parents when they found the parents would not stand firm.

A number of parents in this predicament have found the method of "Logical Consequences" to be superior to the method they have used.[1] If a child doesn't do something his parent asks the child, "Why didn't you...?" or "Why did you..." This procedure makes sense to such a parent because if a product isn't turning out right, you want to know why. The catch is that this procedure doesn't work with children. The usual answer is "I don't know" (a statement that is quite often true). An argument and power struggle ensues, and when the smoke clears away, the child still has usually not done whatever it is he needs to do. The "Why" question is ineffective in changing present behavior.

If a child is required to make his bed in the morning and he doesn't get it done, the parent using logical consequences doesn't interrogate him about his reasons and excuses for not making the bed. But as soon as he gets home from school, he finds that he can't snack or watch TV until he makes his bed. This way is superior to questioning, yelling, and punishing because these activities don't get the bed made. Consequences are logical when they are associated with the behavior that one wants changed.

## The Real vs. the Ideal

Many product-oriented parents, whose eyes are focused firmly on the future instead of what is happening right now, have some ideal in mind. Most of us know what it is to shop around for an "ideal grocery store," "an ideal church," an "ideal school" for our children, or an "ideal community." Finally we give up and settle for a *real* one. The produce department in the grocery store doesn't have fresh lettuce, the church doesn't have a strong adult Sunday school department, the school has classes that are a bit large, and the community doesn't have enough children the age of ours—yet all things considered, these choices were as good as we could make. We finally realized the ideal was only in our *head*; it didn't exist in reality.

The person who is looking for an ideal church or an ideal school has only a very small predicament compared to a person who is looking for an ideal family. A woman looked at her husband to whom she had been married for twenty years and said, "I had hoped to have an ideal marriage." He withered before that remark like a plant in a hot wind. She was a fine Christian person who was having a very difficult time overcoming her tendency to perfectionism. She wanted a perfect marriage, perfect children, and a perfect family. Naturally she did not get them because no real persons could match the ideal in her mind. As she began to work with her predicament, she discovered that a perfectionist (one who is searching for the ideal) is always a gloom-caster. They cast gloom wherever they go because no one is able to live up to the ideal in their minds, not even themselves.

An entirely different kind of adventure, rather than trying to mold our family into some ideal that we have in mind for them, is to nourish them and leave the product up to God. We can build a house according to an ideal—a plan or a blueprint. We can do the same thing with other nonliving things. However, it is not possible to grow even a tree or plant according to an ideal because we never know exactly in what direction they will go, nor how high. The same is true for our children. And perhaps it's better that way. By having this point of view we free them to become all that they are able to become. And we may like the result much better than the "ideal person" we had in our minds.

## Living Now

If you have been worrying about whether your children will turn out all right, has your worrying helped? If

## 241 : IF THEY JUST TURN OUT ALL RIGHT!

you have been looking forward to the day when your children will match the ideal in your mind, has this kept you from enjoying them just like they are, right now? A person who lives in the future is always anxious. As Christians we are concerned about the future. Yet Jesus, who taught so much about the future and made our own future possible, urged his followers to be aware of the present. "Don't be anxious about tomorrow," he taught. "Do not be anxious about your life" (a future-oriented activity) but rather, "Seek first his kingdom [meaning his rule] and his righteousness, and all these things shall be yours as well" (Matthew 6:33). Seeking his rule is a present-oriented activity. The secret is, then, that the future is dependent on focusing on the present. Our children are more likely to "turn out all right" if we play with them, work with them, love them, and resolve predicaments with them *now*.

## Questions

1. Is the time you spend thinking about how your children are going to "turn out" reducing your present involvement with them?
2. Are you able to play with your children just "for the fun of it?"
3. Do you tend to compare your children and your spouse—and yourself—with some "ideal child," "ideal husband or wife," or "ideal self?" If so, is this helping? Can you thank God now for them just as they are?

# NOTES

CHAPTER TWO: PROBLEMS AND PREDICAMENTS
1. I am indebted to the late Dr. Edward John Carnell for differentiating these terms.
2. Omaha (Nebraska) *World-Herald*, May 18, 1975, (AP). Used by permission.

CHAPTER THREE: THE HUMAN PREDICAMENT
1. William Glasser, *The Identity Society*, (New York: Harper & Row, 1971), p. 72.
2. William Glasser, *Reality Therapy*, (New York: Harper Colophon Books, Harper & Row, 1965), p. 51.
3. From the *Good News For Modern Man* version. Used by permission of the American Bible Society, New York, N.Y.
4. Romans 7:15
5. C. S. Lewis, "Essays Presented to Charles Williams," (Grand Rapids: Wm. B. Eerdmans Publishing Co., 1966), Preface pp. XII, XIII. Used by permission.

## CHAPTER FOUR: LEARNING HOW TO DIALOGUE
1. Paul Tournier, *To Understand Each Other*, © M. E. Bratcher, 1967. (Atlanta, Georgia: John Knox Press, 1967), Book Jacket. Used by permission of John Knox Press.
2. Joshua 1:8, 9 (Italics mine).
3. 1 Corinthians 16:13

## CHAPTER FIVE: ANXIETY-RIDDEN THROUGH PRETENDING
1. James 1:7, 8
2. Gunnar Horn (Ed.), *A Cavalcade of British Writing*, (Boston: Allyn & Bacon, 1961), pp. 40-49.
3. *The American Heritage Dictionary of the English Language*, (New York: American Heritage Pub. Co., 1971).
4. O. Hobart Mowrer, *The New Group Therapy*, (Princeton, N.J.: D. Van Nostrand Co., 1964).
5. Arthur Jersild, *When Teachers Face Themselves*, (New York: Teachers' College Press, Columbia University, 1955), Ch. Two. Used by permission.
6. *Ibid.*, p. 35.
7. *Ibid.*, p. 26.
8. Paul Barkman, *Man in Conflict*, (Grand Rapids: Zondervan Pub. House, 1965), p. 67.

## CHAPTER SIX: HUMILITY: AN AID IN REDUCING ANXIETY
1. *The American Heritage Dictionary*, (New York: American Heritage Pub. Co., 1971).
2. Numbers 12:3
3. *Webster's Seventh New Collegiate Dictionary*, (Springfield, Mass.: G. & C. Merriam Co., 1965).
4. I modified this exercise from one used by Dr. Sidney Simon, Prof., University of Massachusetts. The original is reprinted in the Appendix by permission of Hart Publishing Co. The exercise is described in Sidney Simon, Leland W. Howe, and Howard Kirschenbaum, *Values Clarification: A Handbook of Practical Strategies for Teachers and Students*, (New York: Hart Pub. Co., 1972), pp. 30-34, an excellent book of exercises.
5. O. Hobart Mowrer, *The New Group Therapy*, © 1964 by Litton Educational Publishing, Inc. (Princeton, N.J.: D. Van Nostrand Co., 1964), p. 113. Used by permission of D. Van Nostrand Co.
6. *Ibid.*, p. 112.

## CHAPTER SEVEN: JUST AS YOU ARE
1. Carl Rogers, from advertising brochure, "Carl Rogers on Tape," Bell and Howell, 20 Executive Park West, N.E. Atlanta, Georgia 30329 (No date).
2. Luke 19:8
3. R. R. Carkhuff, and B. G. Berenson, *Beyond Counseling and Therapy*, (New York: Holt, Rinehart & Winston, Inc., 1967).

## 245 : NOTES

4. Hebrews 2:18
5. Mark 3:14, (Italics mine).
6. "Prime Time" as a marriage counseling task assignment was introduced to me by Dr. G. B. Dunning, a counseling psychologist from Greenwood, Nebraska.
7. Luke 7:39
8. Luke 7:44-48

### CHAPTER EIGHT: HURT AND ANGER—KNOWING THE DIFFERENCE
1. I am indebted to Dr. G. B. Dunning for teaching me the concept of anger overlaying hurt.

### CHAPTER NINE: A CHRISTIAN—ANGRY?
1. A. T. Jersild, *When Teachers Face Themselves*, (New York: Teachers College Press, 1955), p. 106.
2. *Ibid.*, p. 107.
3. M. Friedman and R. H. Rosenman, *Type A Behavior and Your Heart*, (Greenwich, Connecticut: Fawcett Publications, Inc., © 1974), p. 100. Used by permission of Alfred A. Knopf, Inc.
4. Romans 12:17-19
5. 1 Corinthians 13:5b

### CHAPTER TEN: IF HE'D JUST—ONCE—LISTEN TO ME!
1. Rollo May, *Power and Innocence*, (New York: W. W. Norton & Co., Inc., 1972), p. 23. Used by permission.
2. *Ibid.*, p. 24.
3. Karl Menninger, *Whatever Became of Sin?* (New York: Hawthorne Books, 1973).
4. Herman Melville, *Billy Budd: Sailor*, (Chicago: The University of Chicago Press, 1962).
5. 2 Timothy 3:5
6. Romans 16:25
7. Matthew 7:7
8. Colossians 1:11
9. Philippians 3:10
10. Colossians 1:11

### CHAPTER TWELVE: THE DARK NIGHT OF THE SOUL
1-9. These are excerpts from a counselee's letters, used by permission.

### CHAPTER THIRTEEN: TAKING ACTION
1. Ralph L. Hoy, President, Recordings for Recovery, Box 288, Oakmont, Pa. 15139.
2. Victor E. Frankl, *Psychotherapy and Existentialism: Selected Papers on Logotherapy*, (New York: Simon & Schuster, 1967), p. 27. Used by permission.

3. Bruce Larson, *Living on the Growing Edge*, (Grand Rapids: Zondervan Publishing House, 1968).
4. *Ibid.*, p. 42.
5. Luke 11:24-26
6. Quoted on the cover page of *The American Baptist Magazine*, September 1972, from the book, *Words Are No Good If The Game Is Solitaire*, Copyright 1971, Word Books, Waco, Texas, by Herbert Barks. Used by permission.

## CHAPTER FOURTEEN: THE GIFT OF INVOLVEMENT

1. William Glasser, from tape recording of a speech given in Denver, Colorado, 1969, entitled "Reality Therapy."
2. Sarah Fraser, *Living With Depression–and Winning*, (Wheaton, Ill.: Tyndale House Publishers, Inc., 1975), p. 38. Used by permission.
3. *Webster's Seventh New Collegiate Dictionary*, (Springfield, Mass.: G. & C. Merriam Co., 1965).
4. Donald G. Langsley and David M. Kaplan, *The Treatment of Families in Crisis*, (New York: Grune & Stratton, Inc., 1968), p. 12.
5. *Ibid.*, p. 5, 6.

## CHAPTER FIFTEEN: THREATENED BY THE STRUGGLE

1. "Father and Son," Words and music by Cat Stevens, Copyright 1970 by Freshwater Music Ltd., England. Controlled in Western Hemisphere by Irving Music, Inc. (BMI), Hollywood, Calif., from *Cat Stevens Anthology*, pp. 68-71. All rights reserved. Used by permission. Distributed by Walter Kane & Sons, Inc., 351 West 52nd St., New York, New York, for Triangle Music Corp., 555 Palm Springs Mile, Hialeah, Florida.
2. John Bowlby, *Attachment and Loss, Vol. II: Separation-Anxiety and Anger*, (New York: Basic Books, Inc., 1973), Copyright by the Tavistock Institute of Human Relations.
3. *Ibid.*, p. 253.
4. Robert Manley, "Community Academy Seminar," a mimeographed booklet, 1973.

## CHAPTER SIXTEEN: IT'S HARD TO LET GO!

1. L. Joseph Stone, and Joseph Church, *Childhood and Adolescence*, (New York: Random House, Inc., 1968), p. 16.
2. *Ibid.*, p. 16.
3. Mike Royko, Chicago Daily News Service, "Son's Phone Rings, Rings, Rings—He has Mother Jailed." Used by permission of Mike Royko, *Chicago Daily News*, Chicago, Illinois.
4. James Dobson, *Dare To Discipline*, (Wheaton, Ill.: Tyndale House Publishers, 1970).

# 247 : NOTES

5. Blaise Pascal, *Thoughts and Minor Works*, Vol. 48 of *The Harvard Classics*, (New York: P. F. Collier & Son, 1910), p. 11. Used by permission of Grolier Enterprises, Inc., Danbury, Connecticut.

## CHAPTER SEVENTEEN: IT HELPS TO GET CLOSE IF YOU WANT TO GET AWAY

1. Robert J. Havighurst, *Developmental Tasks and Education*, (Chicago: The University of Chicago Press, 1948).
2. Eric Segal, *Love Story*, (New York: Signet, 1970).

## CHAPTER EIGHTEEN: YOU MEAN A PARENT HAS TO BE A TEACHER, TOO?

1. James Strong, *Strong's Exhaustive Concordance of the Bible*, (New York: Abingdon-Cokesbury, 1890).
2. Albert Einstein, "On Education," from *Human Development: Selected Readings*, (New York: Thomas Y. Crowell Co., 1973). Edited by Morris L. Haimowitz and Natalie Reader Haimowitz, p. 503. This essay is a translation of a speech by Einstein at the tercentenary celebration of higher education in America (Albany, New York, October 15, 1936). Translator: Lina Arronet.
3. Eleanor Estes, *The Middle Moffat*, (New York: Harcourt Brace and Co., 1942).
4. Eleanor Frances Lattimore, *Molly in the Middle*, (New York: William Morrow and Co., Inc., 1965).

## CHAPTER NINETEEN: RECEIVING AND SENDING SILENT SIGNALS

1. Robert Kirkhart and Evelyn Kirkhart, "The Bruised Self: Mending in Early Years," in Kaoru Yamamoto, *The Child and His Image*, (Boston: Houghton Mifflin Co., 1972), pp. 121-177. Used by permission of the publisher.
2. *Ibid.*, p. 152.

## CHAPTER TWENTY: IF THEY JUST TURN OUT ALL RIGHT!

1. The logical consequences method is explained in a step-by-step way in the book, *A New Approach to Discipline: Logical Consequences* by Rudolf Dreikurs and Loren Grey, (New York: Hawthorn Books, Inc., W. Clement Stone, Publisher, 1968). In this excellent paperback book the authors deal with such daily problems as being late to school, doing household chores, leaving toys outside, and fighting.

# INDEX

acceptance, 84, 85
action, 36, 37, 38, 40, 148, 232
advice, 26, 30, 134, 158, 162
ambivalence, 64
appreciation, 176, 195, 197
awareness, 69, 121, 126, 128 (see also sensitivity)
Barkman, Paul, 65
behavior, 37, 61, 62, 74, 77, 130, 148, 226
bibliotherapy, 215
body language, 221, 223, 224, 226, 229, 230 (see also communication, nonverbal)
Bowlby, John, 174
Carkhuff, Robert, 85

communication,
    nonverbal, 59, 220, 223, 226, 228, 230
    verbal, 50, 79, 112, 113, 129, 195, 224, 229
conflict resolution, 175
courage, 73, 113, 232 (see also strength)
courtesy, 132
creativity, 207
defensiveness, 126, 127, 128, 130, 131
despair, 151
determination, 177, 187
developmental tasks, 191
discipline, 139, 204 (see also logical consequences,

250 : INDEX

discipline (*continued*)
    punishment, reward-punishment ratio, and verbal control)
discouragement, 146, 165, 229
Dobson, James, 184
emotional support, 33 (*see also* appreciation)
emotions, see feelings
empathy, 32, 86
enjoyment, 147, 207 (*see also* happiness)
eye contact, 91, 222, 230
failure, 151, 152, 192, 235
fear, 59, 60, 94, 154, 173, 232, 237
feelings, 35, 36, 39, 77, 78, 117, 130, 145, 147, 148, 152, 156, 157, 172
forgiveness, 104, 147
Frankl, Victor, 151, 152
Fraser, Sarah, 161
gentleness, 119
Glasser, William, 36, 61, 161
Graham, Billy, 27, 196
guilt, 54
happiness, 39 (*see also* enjoyment)
Holy Spirit, 118
homework, 214
hopelessness, 138, 162
hospitalization, 140, 164
hostility, 110, 111, 112, 230
Hoy, Ralph, 149
humility, 72, 73, 74, 75
imitation, 204, 205 (*see also* modeling)
intervention, 186, 187
Jersild, Arthur, 62, 65, 110
Jesus, 33, 37, 38, 48, 71, 72, 87, 89, 93, 120, 132, 133, 155, 178, 194, 231, 241
judging others, 31, 84, 85, 110
Kirkhart, Robert and Evelyn, 229
Larson, Bruce, 154
learning channels, 210, 211, 213, 214, 216, 217
  auditory-vocal, 210, 212, 217
  touch-movement, 212, 217
  visual-motor, 210, 212, 217

learning disability, 209, 211
Lewis, C. S., 39
listening, 46, 116, 223, 224
logical consequences, 238, 239
loneliness, 161, 163
love, 89, 109, 113, 114, 139, 155, 156, 164, 181, 221, 231, 241
maternal deprivation, 174
maturity, 100, 101, 105
May, Rollo, 116
meaning, 151, 152, 208
medication, 65, 153
meditation, 51
meekness, 73
Menninger, Karl, 116
mental illness, 165
modeling, 108, 199 (*see also* imitation)
money, 75
moods, 146, 154
motivation, 161
Mowrer, O. Hobart, 61, 75, 76
nonverbal communication, *see* communication
nourishment, 89, 240
observation skills, 47, 70, 126, 221, 223, 225
offense, 109, 113, 114, 221
panic, 29, 92, 94
Pascal, Blaise, 187, 188
peace, 71, 77
playing, 237, 241
possessiveness, 182
power, 116, 117, 118, 119, 120, 123, 231
powerlessness, 115, 116, 119, 129
power struggles, 188, 189, 195
prayer, 52, 104, 110, 184
pretending, 62, 63, 64, 73, 74, 75, 84, 162
pride, 69, 73
prime time, 90
psychoanalysis, 61
punishment, 229, 230 (*see also* discipline)
questioning, 206, 207, 214
reassurance, 30
reconciliation, 196

# INDEX

reinforcement, 208
relationship, 47, 86, 92, 100, 131, 133, 185, 191, 192, 197, 198
resentment, 114, 186
resonating, 43, 46, 189
respect, 190
response length, 49, 50
revenge, 102, 103, 112, 185
reward-punishment ratio, 229
Rogers, Carl, 72, 84
Royko, Mike, 182
runaways, 29, 94, 230
sacrifice, 196
self-depreciation, 138, 139, 143, 155
sensitivity, 121, 122 (*see also* awareness)
sensory-modality, 218 (*see also* learning channels)
separation anger, 185
separation anxiety, 175, 181, 183, 193, 232
separation crisis, 173, 178
sin, 93, 106, 107, 116
singing, 149, 171, 209
St. Francis, 110
strength, 45, 50, 51, 123, 133, 142, 151, 156, 158, 159, 231 (*see also* courage)
success, 151, 152, 192, 235
suicide, 140, 155
task assignments, 92
time investment, 27, 87, 88, 89, 152, 153, 186
touch, 92, 93, 231
Tournier, Paul, 46
values, 82, 192
verbal communication, *see* communication
verbal control, 238
violence, 116
warmth, 20, 42, 45, 232
Wilder, Thornton, 91
Williams, Charles, 39